Malpractice Prevention and Liability Control for Hospitals

James E. Orlikoff
William R. Fifer, M.D.
Hugh P. Greeley

American Hospital Publishing, Inc.,
a wholly owned subsidiary
of the American Hospital Association

AHA®

Library of Congress Cataloging in Publication Data

Orlikoff, James E.
  Malpractice prevention and liability control for hospitals.
  "Catalog no. 178155"—T.p. verso.
  Includes bibliographies.

  1. Hospitals—Administration. 2. Risk management.
3. Hospital care—Quality control. 4. Physicians—
Malpractice. 5. Tort liability of hospitals—United
States. I. Fifer, William R., 1923-   II. Greeley,
Hugh P. III. Title. [DNLM: 1. Hospital administration.
2. Iatrogenic disease—prevention and control.
3. Malpractice. 4. Quality assurance, Health care.
WX 153 071m]
RA971.069   1985   362.1'1'068   85-4063
ISBN 0-939450-62-3   AACR2

Catalog no. 178155

©1981 by American Hospital Publishing, Inc.,
a wholly owned subsidiary of the
American Hospital Association

AHA is a service mark of American Hospital
Association used under license by American
Hospital Publishing, Inc.
3M-8/81-7653
1M-4/85-0082

Contents

List of Figures

List of Tables

CHAPTER 1

Introduction

As the practice of medicine traces its roots to the beginnings of civilization, so, too, does the custom of holding medical practitioners accountable for the care they provide. More than 1,600 years before the drafting of the Oath of Hippocrates (circa 400 B.C), the Code of Hammurabi made provisions for holding physicians accountable for certain injuries they inflicted upon their patients. In perhaps the first definition of medical malpractice and malpractice compensation, the code stated (Kramer, 1976):

> If the surgeon has made a deep incision in the body of a free man and
> has caused the man's death or has opened the caruncle in the eye and
> so destroys the man's eye, they shall cut off his forehand.

One can only speculate about the type of defensive medicine this provision in the code motivated Babylonian physicians to practice, and it is impossible to say how often, if at all, this punishment was imposed.

Yet, from this starting point, the fundamental supposition of physician liability and accountability for iatrogenic patient injury became an integral component of each subsequent society's sanction of medical practice. From Hammurabi's beginning, societies throughout history constructed their own guidelines as to the extent of physician accountability and to the avenues patients might follow to seek redress for their grievances. As civilization and the practice of medicine evolved, the boundaries of physician liability and accountability expanded to include nonphysicians who provide medical care to patients and, further, to include corporate institutions that deliver patient care: hospitals.

Today, if a patient experiences, or thinks he has experienced, an adverse medical event in a hospital, this patient-turned-plaintiff will rarely attempt to hold only a physician liable. A well-known attorney, writing to train other attorneys for the plaintiff in medical malpractice cases, explains this development (Kramer, 1976):

> In most personal injury cases, the plaintiff is usually well advised not to include unnecessary or superfluous party defendants, because it may complicate the likelihood of settlement and adds an unnecessary adversary to attack his claim. However, in a malpractice case, the rule is otherwise, and the plaintiff should include every possible person who might be liable.... Who should be sued?... The answer is to sue both the doctor and the hospital.

If the question "Who should be sued?" were to be asked of physicians, one of the most common and most vehement responses might be "Lawyers!" An article in the *Wall Street Journal* (Aug. 15, 1980) entitled "Doctor vs. Lawyers: After 70,000 Malpractice Actions in Five Years, Physicians Strike Back with Suits of Their Own" points out yet another tangent of the malpractice problem:

> More and more frequently after a disgruntled patient sues—and loses—the doctor countersues. Occasionally he sues the patient. More often he sues the patient's lawyer. In either case, he charges that the original malpractice claim was a frivolous sham that amounted to "malicious prosecution."

It is difficult to imagine whether even Hammurabi himself, the father of bureaucracy, could have envisioned such a pettifogging spate of censorious activity evolving from a well-intentioned law regarding medical malpractice.

To say that the term *medical malpractice* is a contemporary power phrase is to understate the fact. The mere mention of these words can elicit an infinite variety of reactions, from rage to confusion to helplessness and bitterness, depending upon who is being addressed. Many physicians may consider the use of the term tantamount to slander. To hospital administrators, the term may connote large financial losses or exorbitant insurance premiums. Attorneys may regard it as an abstract legal concept or a source of income. To insurance companies, it may mean an actuarial nightmare or the risk of public scrutiny of questionable profits. To patients and the public, medical malpractice can mean anything, including a severe permanent injury or death, a high hospital bill, or any outcome of medical treatment that was less than hoped for. These many meanings and diverse imageries emphasize the numerous economic, political, and human variables entangled within the current phenomenon of medical malpractice and malpractice litigation.

The numerous and various factors that affect or are affected by the malpractice problem lead many contemporary analysts to conclude that this issue, not unlike inflation, is here to stay and likely to get worse.

This conclusion is based on the premise that the overall problem of malpractice is the undesirable but unavoidable result of the interface of such massive systemic variables as the legal system, the medical profession, the economic situation, the insurance industry, and the expectations of the public. Therefore, this reasoning continues, the problem of iatrogenic patient injury culminating in malpractice litigation is incurable and will persist.

This book disagrees with that conclusion. The premise of this book rests upon reducing the supposedly inconceivable—and therefore, irresolvable—etiological variables of malpractice and malpractice litigation to a more understandable form. That premise is simply put: without the occurrence of physician-related patient injury, there should be no significant malpractice litigation problem. Refined to a more operational level, if a hospital can limit the frequency and severity of physician-related patient injury, then it can control and possibly eliminate the occurrence and ramifications of malpractice claims.

What is medical malpractice? What are its legal and conceptual boundaries? What past and present methods are used to control malpractice, and why have they failed? How can physicians and hospitals work together in a purposeful manner to sharply reduce the frequency and severity of patient injury, and thus restrict malpractice claims and liability? It is the purpose of this book to answer these and other critical questions, and to suggest hospital-based strategies and techniques for reducing the incidence of malpractice claims and awards by decreasing the occurrence of physician-related patient injury.

Reference

Kramer, C. *Medical Malpractice*. 4th ed. New York City: Practicing Law Institute, 1976.

CHAPTER 2

The History of Hospital Accountability: from Immunity to Liability

Unlike the long history of physicians' being held accountable for the results of the care they have provided, the chronicles of hospitals' liability and accountability for hospital-based patient care are relatively contemporary. Until recently, most hospitals were protected from corporate liability by the doctrine of charitable immunity. This doctrine, combined with the then pervasive notion that hospitals were just four walls within which physicians treated their patients, gave hospitals almost complete protection from the possibility of corporate liability.

Another historical limitation on hospital corporate liability is related to what is known as the corporate practice doctrine. Historically, state medical practice acts limited licensure of physicians to natural persons only. Hospitals, as corporations, trusts, or other fictitious legal entities, could not practice medicine. Further, because the actions of employees are legally imputed to their employees, hospitals were forbidden from employing physicians.

As a result, to avoid reaching a situation in which a hospital corporation was guilty of an unlicensed practice of medicine in violation of the corporate practice doctrine, and reasoning that corporations cannot regulate the actions of physician-employees in the exercise of their professional judgments as they can regulate the actions of nonprofessional employees, courts considered physicians to be independent contractors to hospitals, rather than employees of them. Yet Willcox (1960) perceived that "some courts have given a large element of flexibility to the corporate practice rule, . . . by taking advantage of the uncertainties inherent in determining whether a particular individual is an employee or an independent contractor."

The combination of these concepts generated a theoretical and organizational separation between the governing body and the medical staff of the hospital. Southwick (1973) points out that "...the role of hospital management was limited to purely financial and housekeeping chores. The practice of medicine was solely a matter for the medical staff physicians."

In its past form, the hospital consisted of two organizations: one that provided hospital services and another that provided medical services. In figure 1, opposite, Caniff (1980) graphically illustrates the dichotomy that existed within hospitals in the past.

As hospitals became more than places of bed and board for the patients of physicians, they gradually lost their status of charitable immunity and began to have imposed upon them the principle of corporate liability. This transition altered the relationship between the governing board and the medical staff of hospitals, as Caniff again illustrates in figure 2, opposite.

THE BASIS OF CORPORATE LIABILITY

Following this transition, a hospital was exposed to corporate liability under two fundamental theories (Cunningham, 1975). The first theory is based on the doctrine of *respondeat superior* ("let the master answer"). The second theory holds that a hospital may be liable if it violates a duty of care that it, as an entity, owes the patient. These two theories require examination in their historical contexts in order to understand the transition of the hospital from charitable immunity to expanding corporate liability.

Respondeat Superior

In 1957, the New York Court of Appeals (Kramer, 1976) ruled that the doctrine of charitable immunity was no longer applicable to hospitals and ruled further that hospitals faced corporate liability under the doctrine of *respondeat superior*. In its decision of *Bing v. Thunig* (1957; Kramer, 1976), the court made the following statement:

> The conception that the hospital does not undertake to treat the patient, does not undertake the act through its doctors and nurses, but undertakes instead simply to procure them to act upon their own responsibility, no longer reflects the fact. Present day hospitals...do far more than furnish facilities for treatment. They regularly employ on a salary basis a large staff of physicians, nurses, and interns, ...and they charge patients for medical care and treatment, collecting for such services, if necessary, by legal action. Certainly, the person who avails himself of "hospital facilities" expects that the hospital will attempt to cure him, not that its nurses or other

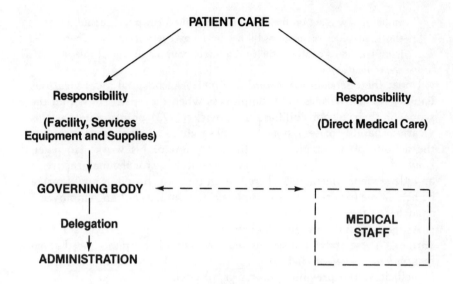

Figure 1
Legal Relationships among the Governing Body, Administration,
and Medical Staff in the Past

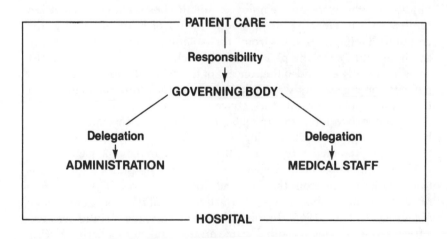

Figure 2
Legal Relationships among the Governing Body, Administration, and
the Medical Staff at the Present Time

employees will act on their own responsibility. Hospitals should, in short, shoulder the responsibilities borne by everybody else. There is no reason to continue their exemption from the universal rule of *respondeat superior.*

Under the doctrine of *respondeat superior,* a hospital faces vicarious liability for the wrongs of its employees when they perform within the scope of their responsibilities. Southwick (1973) points out that this vicarious liability arises from a hospital's right as an employer to regulate the actions of an employee in the execution of his work. However, *respondeat superior* does not hold a hospital liable for the malpractice of an independent contractor. Therefore, in the past, hospitals could rarely be held liable for the actions of a physician who was not an "employee," as such.

As the corporate practice doctrine eroded and the employee status of various "house staff" physicians was recognized, hospitals faced some *respondeat superior* liability for actions of physician-employees. Nonetheless, the prevailing status of physicians remained that of independent contractor, and the limitations of *respondeat superior* insulated hospital from liability for the malpractice of staff physicians.

A Duty of Care

The narrow parameters of *respondeat superior* did not permit any expansion of hospital corporate liability to include the malpractice of staff physicians who were not "employees" of the hospital. This expansion came from a broadening of the second theory of hospital liability: the corporate liability that arises from "the violation of a duty owed directly by the institution to the patient" (Southwick, 1973). A series of court cases has greatly expanded the concept of the hospital's duty of care to its patients and consequently the risk of the hospital's corporate liability. In turn, the application of this concept has begun to alternate the dichotomy between the governing board and the medical staff within the hospital, forcing the relationship between those two bodies to evolve from that represented in figure 1, to that depicted in figure 2, page 7.

The beginning of the movement to expand the hospital's duty of care to the patient came from the Supreme Court of Illinois in 1965 when it ruled on the landmark case of *Darling v. Charleston Community Memorial Hospital (1965).* In this well-known case, the plaintiff suffered a fractured leg during a football game and was taken to Charleston (IL) Community Memorial Hospital's emergency department. Dr. Alexander, the physician on call, applied a cast to plaintiff's fractured leg and admitted him as his patient. It was later noted that Dr. Alexander was not experienced in orthopedic work of this nature. During the plaintiff's stay in the hospital, he repeatedly complained of pain in his leg, and the nurses saw that the toes of the broken leg were insensitive to touch and were blue in color. The plaintiff was later transferred to Barnes Hospital in St. Louis, where his then gangrenous leg was amputated.

In the litigation that followed, Dr. Alexander settled with the plaintiff prior to trial, and the case proceeded to court with the hospital as the only defendant. Plaintiff's complaint, as summarized by Koskoff and Nadeau (1974), alleged that the hospital had been negligent in:

- Permitting the physician to perform orthopedic work of the kind required in this case
- Not requiring the physician to review his operative procedures to bring them up to date
- Failing, through its medical staff, to exercise adequate supervision of the case
- Not requiring consultations, particularly after complications had developed
- Failing to ensure that the nursing staff would report such case development to the hospital administrator
- Not requiring that the administrator call attention to the medical staff and/or that the staff take action with regard to plaintiff's symptoms
- Failing to comply with licensing regulations, accreditation standards, and its own bylaws

The jury found for the plaintiff, and the verdict was later upheld by the Illinois Supreme Court. Although the *Darling* verdict in no way subverted the doctrine of *respondeat superior,* it made it clear that the hospital's liability for Dr. Alexander's negligence was based upon an expansion of the hospital's duty of care. Thus, the predominant basis for hospital corporate liability began to evolve from *respondeat superior* to an expanded duty of care. The *Darling* case specifically expanded the hospital's duty of care to include the following three elements:

1. The hospital must not allow an independent staff physician to violate a specific hospital requirement for patient safety.
2. The hospital must ensure that its employees will detect apparent dangers to the patient and bring such dangers to the attention of the hospital medical or surgical staff and the administration so that the administration can act to alleviate the danger.
3. The hospital has a duty to supervise the actions of independent staff physicians.

The *Darling* case represents a significant turning point in hospital corporate liability for two reasons. First, it set precedent for greatly extending the liability of the hospital by expanding the parameters of the hospital's duty of care to the patient (Southwick, 1973). Second, holding that the standards of the Joint Commission on Accreditation of Hospitals along with the hospital's medical staff bylaws were admissible as evidence for determining negligence, *Darling* also expanded the means available to the plaintiff in establishing the hospital's duty.

Following *Darling*, much confusion was generated regarding the limits of hospital corporate liability arising from the violation of a duty owed to the patient. What duties does the hospital, as an entity, owe the patient? Can we predict how these duties may expand, if at all, over time?

King (1977) addressed these questions by identifying five basic areas of obligation or duty that a hospital owes a patient. Though the duty of the hospital is certainly not limited to the following five areas, King stated that these categories of duty are the ones most often employed by plaintiffs to "support a claim founded on the corporate liability of a hospital in connection with the delivery of medical services":

1. The duty of the hospital to exercise reasonable care in providing proper medical equipment, supplies, medication, and food for its patients
2. The duty of the hospital to exercise reasonable care in providing safe physical premises for its patients
3. The duty of the hospital to adopt internal policies and procedures reasonably estimated to protect the safety and the interests of its patients
4. The duty of the hospital to exercise reasonable care in the selection and retention of hospital employees and in the granting of staff privileges
5. The duty of the hospital to exercise reasonable care to guarantee that adequate patient care is being administered

These duties owed by a hospital to a patient are broad, overlap in certain areas, and are subject to alteration and expansion by case law at any time. They are, however, useful in indicating areas of endeavor that may reduce a hospital's exposure to corporate liability.

The following chapters of this book address liability control and patient safety activities that are specifically directed toward encompassing the last three (and the most difficult) duties of a hospital to patients: policies and procedures to protect the safety and interests of patients, granting of staff privileges, and ensuring that adequate patient care is delivered.

NEGLIGENCE AND MALPRACTICE

In the event that a hospital neglects its duty in any one of these five areas, a suit may be brought against it and others who were involved in providing care to the patient. Any such malpractice lawsuit comes under the category of the civil law and is further divided into one of two categories: contract or tort (King, 1977).

Breach of Contract

Kramer (1976) states that if a physician tells his patient that he will "effect a cure or obtain a specific result and fails to do so," the physician may be liable for breach of contract. Essentially, the dictionary definition of a contract in this context is a guarantee or warranty made by a physician to his patient. Further, breach of contract occurs when a physician (or hospital) has promised a specific result and has failed to deliver. Kramer emphasizes that negligence of the physician or the hospital is *not an issue* in an action for breach of contract.

In the past, physicians were less inhibited about making guarantees to their patients. For this reason, malpractice claims based on breach of contract were more prevalent before 1960 than they are today. However, there is still a propensity for initiating malpractice actions based on contract if the statute of limitations has expired on a possible malpractice action based on tort.

Torts

A tort is any wrongful act that does not involve breach of contract, for which a civil lawsuit can be brought (Prosser, 1971). Tort law is divided into two categories: intentional torts and unintentional torts.

Intentional torts include assault and battery, which, in the medical malpractice context, is the historical basis for suits for lack of informed consent.

Unintentional torts, otherwise known as negligence, constitute the single largest area of malpractice litigation (King, 1977). Negligence is defined by the *Restatement* (1965) as "conduct which falls below the standard established by law for the protection of others against unreasonable risk of harm."

Malpractice / negligence formula

In order to recover in a medical malpractice suit based on negligence, the plaintiff must demonstrate the following four elements (King, 1977):
1. The existence of a standard or duty owed by the physician or hospital to the plaintiff
2. That the standard of care or duty was violated or was not met
3. That the patient-plaintiff sustained a compensable injury
4. That the breach of the standard of care or duty was the proximate cause of the injury

All of the above elements of what Dixon, Lanham, and Ladenburger (1980) term the "malpractice/negligence formula" must be demonstrated for the plaintiff to recover. For example, if the plaintiff in a hypothetical malpractice suit based on negligence can demonstrate the first three elements but cannot demonstrate that the breach of duty *caused* the injury, then the plaintiff will not recover and the defendant will prevail. Likewise, a plaintiff will be unsuccessful in recovering if there is no compensable or measurable harm or injury (Dixon, Lanham, and Ladenburger, 1980). Although injury in itself is perhaps the easiest component of the malpractice/negligence formula to demonstrate, its existence can be ambiguous and difficult to prove in cases in which the plaintiff tries to demonstrate psychological damage.

Conversely, the second component of the formula (breach of duty) is often ambiguous and difficult for the plaintiff to demonstrate. King (1977) states that the breach of duty for any case is usually defined by expert medical testimony. Often, the expert testimony given for the plaintiff is contradicted by expert testimony given for the defendant. The decision of the court will often be based upon the relative merits of the expert testimony and upon the qualifications of the expert giving testimony. This is, perhaps, the primary reason behind the many different judgments handed down by the courts in cases of similar circumstance. The breach of duty must not always be defined by medical expert testimony, however; the plaintiff may, in certain cases, rely upon the doctrine of *res ipsa loquitur.*

Proof in the circumstances

Res ipsa loquitur (Latin for "the thing speaks for itself") is a doctrine based upon circumstantial proof. Under this doctrine, one of the most commonly misunderstood, the plaintiff attempts to demonstrate that the nature of the injury itself is sufficient to suggest a breach of duty. That the physician or hospital (defendant) caused the injury (the fourth element of the malpractice/negligence formula) can be proved circumstantially, by *res ipsa loquitur.* As King (1977) points out, "Where the existence of an injury is sufficient to support an inference that the standard of care has been violated, it will often support an inference that the supposed negligence caused the injurious occurrence."

The three classic and often cited conditions for the application of *res ipsa loquitor* are that " (1) the accident must be of a kind which ordinarily does not occur in the absence of someone's negligence: (2) it must be caused by an agency or instrumentality within the exclusive control of the defendant: (3) it must not have been due to any voluntary action or contribution on the part of the plaintiff" (*Ybarra v. Slangard* [1944] 25 Cal. 2d 486, 489, 154 P.2d 687).

In a recent decision (Kolakowski v. Viris; *Occurrence*, 1981), the Illinois Supreme Court espoused the logic for the extension of hospital corporate liability under the legal doctrine of *res ipsa loquitur* in cases of surgery in which the patient receives general anesthesia. The court stated, "When a patient submits himself of the care of a hospital and its staff and is rendered unconscious for the purpose of surgery performed by independent contracting surgeons, the control necessary under *res ipsa loquitur* will have been met. The burden will then shift to the hospital to dispel the inference that it exercised the control necessary to the application of *res ipsa loquitur.*"

Another method is available to the plaintiff to prove that a standard of care that was violated caused the injury, although it is not uniformly applied. Under this method, the plaintiff may rely upon an admission from the physician or hospital that "a mistake was made" or on any other duly witnessed statement that implies breach of duty and causation of injury.

Informed consent

Another area of malpractice litigation that has received increased attention is informed consent. Historically, medical consents were required merely as a granting of permission by a patient or the patient's legal representative for a technical assault or battery upon the patient (Ludlam, 1978). Prosser (1971) notes that "the gist of the action for battery is not the hostile intent of the defendant, but rather the absence of consent to the contact on the part of the plaintiff."

The modern action for informed consent, as Ludlam notes, has grown to encompass two distinct legal theories, battery *and* negligence. "The battery theory should be reserved for those circumstances when a doctor performs an operation to which the patient has not consented. When the patient gives permission to perform one type of treatment and the doctor performs another, the requisite element of deliberate intent to deviate from the consent given is present. However, when the patient consents to certain treatment and the doctor performs that treatment but an undisclosed inherent complication with a low probability occurs, no intentional deviation from the consent given appears; rather, the doctor in obtaining consent may have failed to meet his due care duty to disclose pertinent information. In that situation, the action should be pleaded in negligence" (*Cobbs v. Grant*, 1972).

From the plaintiff's perspective, the advantage of suing for battery is that medical expert testimony is not necessary to the success of the case, as it is in a negligence suit. Also, because local statutes of limitations may provide the plaintiff with a longer period of time to sue for battery than to sue for medical malpractice, the battery theory may be advantageous for suits initiated after considerable time has expired since the injury.

The preceding has been a brief analysis of negligence and malpractice from the legal perspective. Malpractice laws vary significantly from state to state, and a local attorney certainly should be consulted when specific legal questions exist. Yet, in order to better understand the problem as a whole and its causes, and so to minimize them, it is conceptually useful to consider a more inclusive model of the interaction among patient injury, negligence, and liability. Don Harper Mills, a principal investigator for the California Medical Insurance Feasibility Study (California Medical Association, 1977), developed the model that appears in figure 3, below.

As a supplement to the malpractice/negligence formula, this model is useful as a reminder that all medically caused patient injuries do not necessarily equal legal liability or actual malpractice. The model also points out that each instance of "legal fault" (or breach of a standard of care) does not always result in injury to the patient, and therefore does not complete the malpractice/negligence formula. Conceptually, then, it is the intersection of medically caused patient injuries with the incidence

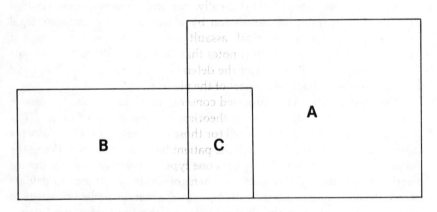

Figure 3
The Relationship of Patient Injury to Negligence and Liability

Box A represents the total incidence of medically caused patient injuries. Box B represents the incidence of legal fault by members of the health care professions (for example, carelessness, failure to disclose risks for consent purposes, or failure to warn or instruct patients) without the occurrence of patient injuries. The overlap of boxes A and B (area C) constitutes the theoretical incidence of legal liability in our present fault system of litigation (that is, legal fault is responsible for those medically caused injuries).

of legal fault that equals compensable negligent malpractice. Chapter 3 discusses the scope of the problem that this intersection represents—not only its frequency in the past two decades but also the variety of factors that have influenced the increase in claims of medical malpractice.

References

Bing v. Thunig 2 N.Y. 2d 656, 143 N.E. 2d3, 163 N.Y.S. 2d3 (1957).

California Medical Association. *Report on the Medical Insurance Feasibility Study.* San Francisco: CMA, 1977.

Caniff Jr., C.E. Responsibilities and relationships of the medical staff, administration, and governing body. Presented at the American Medical Association seminar, Medical staff: Physician, friend, or foe, Chicago, Apr. 24, 1980.

Cobbs v. Grant, 8 Cal. 3d 229, 502 P. 2d 1 (1972).

Cunningham, J.D. The hospital-physician relationship: hospital responsibility for malpractice of physicians. *Wash. Law Rev.* 50:385, 1975.

Darling v. Charleston Community Memorial Hospital, 33 Ill. 2d 326, 211 N.E. 2d 253 (1965), *cert. denied* 383 U.S. 946 (1966).

Dixon, N., and others *Quality, Trending, and Management for the '80s.* Chicago: American Hospital Association, 1980.

King Jr., J.H. *The Law of Medical Malpractice in a Nutshell.* St. Paul: West Publishing Co., 1977.

Koskoff, T.I., and Nadeau, T.L. Hospital liability: the emerging standard of care. *Conn. Bar J.* 48: 305, Sept. 1974.

Kramer, C. *Medical Malpractice.* New York City: Practicing Law Institute, 1976.

Ludlam, J.E. *Informed Consent.* Chicago: American Hospital Association, 1978.

Norvell, P.E. Torts: the expanding liability of hospitals. *Okla. Law Rev.* 26: 441, Aug. 1973.

Occurrence. Chicago, Mar.-Apr. 1981.

Prosser, W.L. *The Law of Torts* (Hornbook Series). 4th ed. St. Paul: West Publishing Co., 1971, pp. 36 and 458-460.

Restatement 2d, Torts 282 (1965).

Southwick, A.F. The hospital as an institution—expanding responsibilities change its relationship with the staff physician. *Calif. West. Law Rev.* 9: 429, Spring 1973.

Willcox, A.W. Hospitals and the corporate practice of medicine. *Cornell Law Rev.* 45: 432, 1960.

Ybarra v. Slangard (1944) 25 Cal. 2d 486, 489 [154 P. 2d 687].

CHAPTER 3

Dissecting the Malpractice Problem

As the first chapter in this book states, society's recognition of, and its attempts to deal with, the possibility of medical malpractice can be traced at least as far back as the Code of Hammurabi, at which time such a transgression could have cost a surgeon the use of his hand. However, society's consideration of malpractice as a problem of crisis-like proportions is relatively new; 90 percent of all suits in the United States have been filed since 1964 (Salmon, 1979). The cost of malpractice, on the other hand, has changed only in kind; physicians are spending more than one billion dollars a year on malpractice insurance, and hospitals are paying twice that amount (*U.S. News and World Report*, 1978).

SCOPE OF THE PROBLEM

Costs for malpractice insurance have risen to these levels in direct relationship to the sudden increase in malpractice claims filed since 1964. The National Association of Insurance Commissioners (NAIC) reported 24,158 closed claims against physicians and hospitals (14,074 of which were against physicians) during the period from July 1, 1975, to June 30, 1976 (*Amer. Medical News*, 1978). This figure does not represent the total number of either incidents or claims in that year, as there is a time lag of 21 months between the date of an incident, or adverse patient occurrence, and the date a claim is reported to an insurance company; furthermore, an average of 34 months elapses between an incident and the closure (payment) of a claim (*Parthenon*, 1979).

As early as 1970, according to the Department of Health, Education, and Welfare (now Department of Health and Human Services) Secretary's Commission, 26,500 physicians were sued (*Amer. Medical News*, 1978), which represents about seven malpractice claims for every

100 active practitioners (Brook and Williams, 1978). However, the number of lawsuits alleging malpractice or professional liability is probably only the tip of the iceberg: Pocincki (1973) says that only one in 15 patients who sustain "severe injury" sues; for example, only 4,000 claims were filed in California in 1974, the same year in which 24,000 "potentially compensable events" were predicted on the basis of data demonstrated by the California Medical Insurance Feasibility (CMIF) Study (Schwartz and Komesar, 1978).

Similarly, Roger O. Egeberg, M. D., former special consultant to the President for health, estimated that two million medical injuries occur in the United States annually, of which 700,000 appear to involve some negligence. Yet only 20,000 claims are made per year (Somers, 1977). The Institute of Medicine report (1978) states "the incidence of medical injury is unknown," and cites reported incidences of 5 percent, 8 percent, and 11 percent.

As figure 3, page 14, indicates, one must distinguish clearly between patient injury, negligence, and liability, the latter being the simultaneous occurrence of patient injury and negligence. In the CMIF Study (California Medical Assn., 1977), Mills found, through peer review of a randomly selected sample of more than 20,000 hospital records, a 4.65 percent incidence of patient injury, of which 17 percent (0.8 percent of the total) was thought to be due to negligence. By extrapolating from the CMIF Study findings, one could predict a total of 140,000 "potentially compensable events" in all California hospitals in 1974, of which 23,800 would result in liabilities and 13,600 would result in death.

In addition to these alarming frequency data, evidence suggests that the problem is increasing. The Saint Paul Companies, which insure 35,000 physicians and 1,400 hospitals, reported that between 1970 and 1976 claims filed against insureds rose 20 percent per year (*Amer. Medical News*, 1978). Although the incidence of claims dropped 11 percent between 1975 and 1976, the Saint Paul Fire and Marine Insurance Company reported a dramatic increase in both the frequency and severity of claims reported in 1978 (*Minnesota Medical Newspage*, 1979).

The chances of an individual physician being sued have been variously estimated (*Amer. Medical News*, 1978). In 1974, 10 percent of all Saint Paul physician policy holders were involved in a claim, and the NAIC data show 14,074 closed claims from July 1, 1975, to June 30, 1976, which represents 4.5 percent of the 311,937 physicians involved in patient care as of December 31, 1975. The AMA Center for Health Services Research reports that one of eight U.S. physicians (12.9 percent) has been sued within the three-year period from 1974 to 1976.

As if the frequency and increase in the problem were not enough, there is clear evidence that the severity of the problem—as defined by the size of the claims—is increasing (*Amer. Medical News*, 1978). The Saint Paul Companies reported an increase of 15 percent in the average value of claims from 1975 to 1976, during which period the NAIC reported a 12.6 percent increase in average dollar amount. In dollars, the increase per award was reported to be from $148,456 in 1976 to $197,533 in 1977. In California, where the cost of professional liability coverage resulted in a work stoppage among anesthesiologists in 1975, the average award rose from $123,000 in 1976 to $262,000 in 1977 (Los Angeles County). The California Medical Association found a 72.3 percent increase in the dollar amount of claims from 1976 to 1977.

A high number of claims, of course, does not equate with high dollar awards (*Amer. Medical News*, 1978). The NAIC reported that, of 14,074 claims against physicians, 9,018 (64 percent) resulted in no dollar award; of the remainder, only 245 (5 percent) resulted in awards exceeding $100,000. The spectacular, million-dollar suits occurred only 11 times in 1977. An HEW survey of closed claims reported the average malpractice award in 1976 to be $27,708 (*Parthenon*, 1979), almost double the value of $14,281 paid in 1970 (*Amer. Medical News*, 1979). Although permanent total disability resulted in large awards (average $145,275 in 1976), the average paid claim against a physician was only $17,676 in 1976 (*Amer. Medical News*, 1978).

CAUSES OF THE PROBLEM

From whichever point one views these figures, they are cause for alarm, because they represent not only a great financial burden for health care practitioners and institutions but also injury to patients and higher costs of care for all health care consumers. Any attempt to ameliorate the problem must, of course, examine its causes. Clearly, the problem of malpractice claims is not confined to any single variable, such as the practice of medicine within hospitals or the changing legal theories of hospital corporate liability. Rather, malpractice litigation and its many ramifications find their root causes in the intersection of numerous generic variables, as a review of the theories proposed by various authors demonstrates.

Brook (1978), for example, contends that "Malpractice claims are almost always rooted in medical injury and poor practice; they are not often produced by the whim of a hysterical person."

Salmon (1979) advances the following theories of the causes of malpractice:

• Increased availability of health care
• Consumers' view of health care as a product

- Patients' awareness of their rights
- Breakdown of the physician-patient relationship
- High consumer expectations
- Inevitability
- Lack of informed consent

In contrast, Curran (1979) describes lack of informed consent as a "mythical" cause of malpractice suits, based on the fact that it was alleged in only 2.5 percent of the Saint Paul 1973-78 cases. He describes "abandonment" (when one physician takes himself off a case without confirming that another physician has replaced him) as another myth, which explains only 0.8 percent of the cases.

The Institute of Medicine report (1978) discusses some generic hypothetical causes of the malpractice problem:

- Lawyers
- Litigiousness
- Medical care
- Poor rapport
- Cost (including size of physician incomes)
- Insurance crisis

It can be inferred from this list that medical care itself leads to at least the potential for malpractice suits, in the sense that it is a necessary precondition. Although no one seriously advocates the cessation of medical care as a solution to the malpractice litigation problem, a practitioner may elect the safer of two alternatives in dealing with a patient's problem: for example, arthritis of the hip can be more "safely" treated with aspirin than with surgical total hip replacement. The DHEW Secretary's Commission on Medical Malpractice (1973) concluded that "malpractice claims are actually rooted in medical injury and malpractice" (Somers, 1977).

Vaccarino (1978) describes three situations as precursors to a suit and, therefore, as generic causes of liability: (1) a poor physician-patient relationship, (2) a poor result of care, and (3) an excessive bill. Like other authors, he believes that the "malpractice crisis" has multiple roots and cites litigiousness, a crisis of expectations, an insurance industry crisis, and malpractice as the four major causes. Vaccarino states further that "the act of ordinary negligence (malpractice), which will occur with statistical surety in a random fashion in all our daily lives, can only be prevented by diligent conduct—by the practice of good medicine."

The Parthenon Insurance Company (1979) has a somewhat different view of the generic causes of malpractice, listing the following:

- Inadequate communication
- Inadequate medical records

- Human and equipment systems failures
- Poor judgment by those providing health services

In this same vein—of ascribing the incidence of malpractice claims at least in part to the inefficiencies of the medical care system—Fifer describes the relatively new function of hospital risk management as "the art of preventing people failure" (1977), and other authors define hospital risk management as "a detection system designed to predict when the next system or person will fail and to prevent it from happening" (Hirsch and White, 1978).

Experts agree that in malpractice cases the content, quality, completeness, and consistency of the medical record are critical. (*The Record That Defends Its Friends*, 1979). "When a record has been tampered with . . . the insurance company will almost invariably settle," rather than risk a greater financial loss in court.

Finally, the American Bar Association *Report of the Commission on Medical Professional Liability* (1977) lists the following as contributors to the increase in liability:

- The growth in medical technology
- Involvement of more personnel in the treatment sequence
- An increased readiness of patients to question experts and expertise
- Inadequate efforts by hospitals to prevent adverse incidents
- Inadequate medical discipline
- Liberal courts
- More lawyers
- Rapid escalation in the dollar amount of damages

This list introduces several ideas not obvious from previous lists: among them, that "medical discipline" is lax, and that hospital efforts to prevent adverse patient occurrences, or incidents, are inadequate. Similarly, charging the former cause, Somers (1977) discusses the "impaired physician" as a factor in negligent care and lauds present efforts by state medical associations to deal with the problem. He also cites the current wave of licensure reform activities (such as mandatory relicensure usually accompanied by a continuing education requirement) as potentially valuable in enhancing medical discipline. In contrast, Somers discounts the "too many lawyers" hypothesis on the grounds that lawyers reject 88 percent of all cases brought to them and that most reputable lawyers would not proceed with a suit unless a medical consultant's review of the case concluded that both negligence and causal relationship to harm were apparent.

This great variety of sometimes conflicting theories of the etiology of the malpractice litigation problem can be simplified somewhat, depending on how the problem is defined:

- If, for example, the problem is defined in terms of the frequency of patient injury, one set of explanations seems most plausible, on the basis of deficiencies in the delivery of medical care and on the rapidly increasing sophistication and availability of medical technology and practice.
- If the problem is defined in terms of the frequency of lawsuits against health care providers, another set of explanations is invoked. Among these are the current general mistrust of experts and expertise; the contradictory but nonetheless present and unreasonably high expectations of consumers in the power of modern medicine, undoubtedly generated by popular communications media; the rise of the "consumer rights" movement, which has encouraged a climate of litigiousness that affects professions other than health care and that has produced a great rise in the product liability experienced by manufacturers; and the legal system and the rapidly increasing number of attorneys who specialize in malpractice litigation on the contingency fee system.
- Finally, if malpractice is considered a problem because of the costliness or unavailability of professional liability insurance, then its cause is related to the decisive role that the insurance industry played in the malpractice crisis and the manner in which it continues to affect the malpractice climate.

ROLE OF THE INSURANCE INDUSTRY

Upon the surface, the malpractice crisis of 1973-75 was one of rapidly escalating medical professional liability insurance (malpractice insurance) costs combined with prolonged malpractice insurance unavailability. The crisis was aggravated by the increasing incidence of medical malpractice claims and awards. Yet of these three variables, two of them—escalating malpractice insurance costs and the increasing incidence of malpractice claims and awards—were not sudden occurrences, popular opinion notwithstanding.

The incidence of malpractice claims filed and the dollar amounts of damages sought and awarded had been significantly increasing since the mid-1960s. The average premium paid by hospitals and physicians for malpractice insurance quadrupled from 1960 to 1970 (Guinther, 1978). Yet these critical variables in and of themselves were insufficient justification for public or professional pronouncement of a "malpractice crisis." This concern about litigation was of primary interest to physicians and hospitals and generated little or no anxiety for the insurance industry, even as late as 1973. In fact, the medical malpractice commission of DHEW reported in 1973 that insurers were still very interested in the malpractice liability field for several reasons, the major one being that they regarded "the prevailing level of premium rates . . . as adequate" to their needs (Guinther, 1978).

In late 1973, the insurers recognized that the malpractice claims they were seeing and settling were but a small portion of the total number of iatrogenic injuries or "potentially compensable events" that occurred each year (California Medical Association, 1977). This knowledge com-pelled the insurers to logically conclude that the potential increase in claims filed from one year to the next was unpredictable. Unpredictabil-ity is perhaps the single greatest source of discomfort to insurance com-panies, as their profits depend upon the accuracy of their predicted losses. Guinther (1978) succinctly sums up the problem then facing the insurers:

> The insurers (became aware) that the 10-15 percent claims rise they
> had been seeing might be nothing more than the tip of the iceberg.
> This year, next year, or the one after that could see claims rise by 100
> percent or 200 percent or some incalculable percent, causing the in-
> dustry to face billions of dollars in claims payments at a time when it
> was earning premiums only in the hundreds of millions.

The concern about malpractice litigation was now on its way to be-coming a crisis.

Another variable fueled the fire of the impending crisis: 1973 saw the beginning of an economic recession that imperiled the investments of the insurers (the insurers invested in common stocks and other ventures from their cash held in reserve to pay predicted losses due to claims). Several authors (Guinther, 1978; Lander, 1978; Somers, 1977) compellingly con-tend that the malpractice claims crisis was borne by the insurer's cognizance of the unpredictability of the potential future rise in claims in combination with a deteriorating economy that threatened their profits and solvency.

The insurance carriers, in late 1973 and early 1974, responded to this situation in one of two ways: sudden and total withdrawal from the malpractice insurance market; or, for those insurers that remained in the market, astronomical premium rate increases for hospitals and physi-cians, without increasing coverage. Guinther (1978), in support of the first point, states that the number of insurers underwriting statistically significant amounts of malpractice insurance fell from 25 to 12 between 1973 and 1975. Brown (1979), demonstrating the second point, identified the case of one hospital's malpractice insurance premium increase from 79 cents per patient day in 1974 to $11.20 per patient day in 1977 for comparable coverage.

Hospitals and physicians responded with outrage to the actions of the insurers. Lander (1978) quotes the Physicians Crisis Committee of Detroit, which somewhat tendentiously stated in 1975:

> The insurance industry, with a few exceptions, has failed miserably in representing both physicians and the public . . . Instead of proposing solutions when the going got hot, *the industry turned and ran.* (Emphasis in the original.) Of little concern to them was the fact that doctors would be left totally unprotected and that society would be left without physicians to care for them.

Amid these torrents of accusations and general murmurs of disaffection, hospitals and physicians were forced to explore alternatives to traditional malpractice insurance as well as to investigate new methods of mediating the problem. Dixon (1980) contends that one immediate result of the malpractice crisis was the sudden plunge of hospitals into the insurance business. Indeed, the very costly or, in some areas, completely unavailable professional liability insurance from commercial sources led to widespread self-insurance by hospitals, hospital associations, and medical societies or their "captives." By the end of 1979, 21 percent of the nation's nonfederal, acute care beds were insured by captives, a 75 percent increase from 12 percent in 1977 (*Reciprocal News,* 1979).

This move by hospitals and physicians to self-insurance was an immediate and necessary response to the risks that lack of coverage posed in the wake of the first malpractice crisis. It was, and continues to be, one method of controlling that set of causes of the malpractice problem that are related to the insurance industry. Another response was the development and initiation of the hospital-based function of risk management, which includes risk financing as well as loss prevention and control. Hospital risk management was designed to deal with another set of causes—those deficiencies in the medical care delivery system that were resulting in patient injury. The following chapter discusses both of these responses and their effectiveness in greater detail.

References

American Bar Association. *1977 Report of the Commission on Medical Professional Liability.* Chicago: ABA, 1977.

Amer. Medical News, Chicago, Apr. 28, 1978.

Amer. Medical News, Chicago, June 29, 1979.

Brook, R.H., and Williams, K.N. Malpractice and the quality of care. *Ann. Intern. Med.* 88:836, 1978.

Brown Jr., B.L. *Risk Management for Hospitals: A Practical Approach.* Germantown, MD: Aspen Systems Corporation, 1979.

California Medical Association. *Report on the Medical Insurance Feasibility Study.* San Francisco: CMA, 1977.

Curran, W.J. Malpractice claims: new data and trends. *New Engl. J. Med.* 300:26, 1979.

Dixon, N. Conventional risk management systems and what's wrong with them. Presented at the University of Minnesota continuing medical education program: *Primum Non Nocere.* Minneapolis, Mar. 28-29, 1980.

Fifer, W.R. Risk management: the art of preventing 'people failure.' *Trustee.* 30:52, 1977.

Guinther, J. *The Malpractitioners.* New York City: Anchor Press/Doubleday, 1978.

Hirsch, H.L., and White, E.R. Risk management: preventive medicine for malpractice. *Hosp. Med. Staff.:* 1, October 1978.

Institute of Medicine, National Academy of Sciences. *Beyond Malpractice: Compensation for Medical Injuries, A Policy Analysis* (Publication no. 78-01). Washington, DC: National Academy of Sciences, Mar. 1978.

Lander, L. *Defective Medicine: Risk, Anger, and the Malpractice Crisis.* New York City: Farrar, Strauss, and Giroux, 1978.

Minnesota Medical NewsPage, St. Paul, Jan. 1979.

Parthenon Insurance Company Newsletter, Nashville, Jan.-Feb. 1979.

Parthenon Insurance Company Newsletter, Nashville, Mar.-Apr. 1979.

Parthenon Insurance Company Newsletter, Nashville, May-June 1979.

Pocincki, L.S., and others. The incidence of iatrogenic injuries. In Department of Health, Education, and Welfare, *Report of the Secretary's Commission on Medical Malpractice.* Washington, D.C.: Government Printing Office (DHEW #0573-89), 1973, pp 50-70.

Reciprocal News, Richmond, VA, Mar.-Apr. 1979.

Salmon, S.L. A systems approach can ensure high-quality care and low costs. *Hospitals.* 53:79, Mar. 16, 1979.

Schwartz, W.B., and Komesar, N.K. Doctors, damages, and deterrence—an economic view of medical malpractice. *New Engl. J. Med.* 298:1282, 1978.

Somers, H.M. The malpractice controversy and the quality of patient care. *Milbank Mem. Fund O.* 55:193, Spring 1977.

The Record that Defends Its Friends. Chicago: Care Communications, Inc., 1979.

U.S. News and World Report. 85:50, Dec. 4, 1978.

Vaccarino, J.M. Malpractice: the problem in perspective. *J. Amer. Med. Assoc.* 238:861, 1978.

CHAPTER 4

Hospitals' Response: Insurance Options and Risk Management

As chapter 3 suggests, the malpractice crisis painfully pointed out that several alternative malpractice insurance options are available to hospitals. Prior to choosing an alternative insurance option, however, hospitals must become familiar with certain fundamental concepts of insurance. The American College of Surgeons (1979) succinctly reminds us that the purpose of malpractice liability insurance is to transfer ". . . the financial consequences of risk from the hospital to another carrier—in effect, spreading the risk over a larger group and thereby, theoretically, decreasing the financial consequences to each member of the group."

DEVELOPMENT OF INSURANCE ALTERNATIVES

Malpractice insurance policies generally take one of two forms: claims-made policies or occurrence policies (American College of Surgeons, 1979). The occurrence policy is the most common policy of commercial malpractice insurance and provides coverage for liability arising from malpractice that occurred while the policy was in effect. For example, if a claim is filed after an occurrence policy has expired, but the claim alleges an act of malpractice that occurred when the policy was in force, the occurrence policy will cover the management and payment of the claim. The delay between an actual incident of malpractice and the filing of the claim is called the *long tail*. For an insurance company underwriting occurrence policies, the long tail means that the insurer will be covering claims many years after the policy has expired. In contrast, the claims-made policy covers only those claims that are actually made during the tenure of the policy. For obvious reasons, commercial insurance carriers are more inclined to write claims-made policies rather than occurrence policies.

Hospitals are not limited to these two choices offered by traditional malpractice insurance coverage, however. The literature suggests many alternatives to commercial insurance available to hospitals (American College of Surgeons, 1979; Brown, 1979; Kucera and Ator, 1978; Tanenbaum and Korsak, 1978). Some of the most commonly employed alternatives include:

- *Joint underwriting associations.* Brown (1979) states that these associations were formed to force commercial insurers to provide malpractice insurance to those hospitals unable to obtain coverage. "The joint underwriting association acts as an underwriting agent for the commercial underwriters or, alternatively, may reinsure existing policies of underwriters who do not wish to accept business."
- *Captive insurance companies.* Kucera and Ator (1978) state that the captive is a "wholly owned subsidiary of a group of participating hospitals organized for the purpose of insuring their risks. In essence, it is a self-insurance program which has taken on all the formalities of an insurance company."
- *Funded self-insurance.* This alternative insurance method retains the risk within the hospital or group of hospitals while providing a funding mechanism (similar to a trust fund) to cover the cost of litigation and malpractice liability losses.
- *Nonfunded self-insurance, or "going bare."* Kucera and Ator (1978) point out that, under this method, the hospital makes no prearrangement whatsoever for the payment of malpractice liability losses or litigation or claims management costs. Rather, the hospital pays its malpractice losses and related expenses from its operating capital.

Each of these alternatives has its own advantages and disadvantages, with the possible exception of the fourth, "going bare," which has many disadvantages and few discernible advantages. Kucera and Ator state that going bare can best be described as "imprudent management." Table 1, page 30, displays certain relative advantages and disadvantages of the insurance options discussed.

PAST AND CURRENT ATTEMPTS TO MANAGE PREDICTABLE LOSS

In addition to being forced to search out or create viable alternatives to commercial malpractice insurance, hospitals began to actively engage in certain internal activities that, in the past, had been delegated to the insurers. Primary among these activities was one that became known as risk management.

Risk management is a term that was popularized in 1963 by two professors of insurance, Mehr and Hedges (1963). Risk management refers to minimizing or financing, through insurance, predictable losses in business. Orlikoff and Lanham (1980) state that the term *risk management* has taken on a more focused meaning for hospitals—encompassing prediction of risk of patient injury, avoidance of exposure to predicted and other risks, and minimization of malpractice claims loss.

Prior to the malpractice crisis, hospitals had not been performing internal risk management functions. Rather, these risk management functions, which primarily included claim surveillance and management, incident investigation, and equipment safety, had been assumed by the commercial insurance carriers as conditions of coverage (American College of Surgeons, 1978; Brown, 1979).

Hospitals were forced to begin developing their own internal risk management programs in the mid-1970s as a basic response to the malpractice crisis. Additionally, the majority of the malpractice insurance alternatives (including those commercial insurers who continued to offer coverage after the malpractice crisis of 1974-75) required, as a condition of coverage, that hospitals develop their own formal internal risk management programs. Dixon (1980a) maintains that, from this initial impetus, hospital risk management programs evolved following one of two conceptual models. These two models are the safety model and the patient injury model. Table 2, page 32, presents an initial comparison of the salient points of the two risk management models.

As table 2 indicates, both models of risk management have points of convergence as well as divergence. Both models recognize risk management as a necessary hospital activity to minimize loss. At the conceptual level, both models are grounded in the assumption that active, purposeful involvement in the investigation and prevention of patient injuries will increase each hospital's sensitivity to the societal variables that influence the malpractice litigation climate and generate malpractice crises. The patient injury model, however, is conceptually more complete than the safety model because it emphasizes the importance of continually striving to improve the quality of patient care (as opposed to solely attempting to reduce patient injuries) as concomitant to a functioning risk management program.

Aside from conceptual differences, the two models of risk management also differ in their functional methods and techniques. Perhaps the most significant difference between the two is that the patient injury model requires active review of both the medical practice and the medical staff of a hospital as an integral component of the risk management system. The patient injury model also emphasizes reliance on communication with hospital quality assurance activities to help identify

TABLE 1
Comparison of Various Forms of Malpractice Liability Insurance*

Type of Insurance	Advantages	Disadvantages
Commercial insurance	1. Transfers liability for catastrophic loss to another party. 2. May give hospital the services of an experienced risk management and claims investigation/defense team. 3. More "comfortable" than other alternatives.	1. Cost of premiums may sharply exceed hospital's own loss experience. 2. Cost of agent/broker commissions. 3. Limited incentive for hospital to control risks. 4. Future malpractice crises may induce the insurer to suddenly withdraw from the market.
Joint underwriting associations	1. By acting as an underwriting agent or reinsurer, such associations can provide an insurance market where no other market exists.	1. Limited coverage is subject to rigid terms. 2. Limited excess insurance is available through commercial carriers. 3. Limited risk management services are available. 4. Temporary measure only; will not provide long-term solutions to hospital's insurance problems.

Captive insurance companies	1. Pooling risks stabilizes costs. 2. Larger limits of liability possible. 3. Can be less expensive than commercial or self-insurance. 4. Hospitals can benefit from the risk management experiences of other participating hospitals.	1. Gaining consensus on captive's goals and strategies can be difficult. 2. Obtaining initial financing sufficient to cover all members can be difficult. 3. Possible inefficient operation due to inexperience.
Funded self-insurance	1. Can be less expensive if hospital can predict and control risks effectively. 2. Provides definite incentives for hospital to prevent and control risks. 3. Risk management program can be fine-tuned to the needs of the hospital.	1. Hospital must assess its own risks. 2. Excess liability insurance may be difficult to obtain. 3. Complex accounting problems, especially given the possibility of "once in a lifetime claims." 4. Mechanisms must conform to third-party payer guidelines in order to receive reimbursement.
Nonfunded self-insurance (going bare)	1. May be a necessary alternative for hospitals with severe cash flow problems.	1. A single successful claim, or a series of claims, could bankrupt the hospital.

*Adapted, with permission, from the American College of Surgeons *Patient Safety Manual*, 1979.

TABLE 2
Comparison of the Safety and Patient Injury Models of Risk Management*

	Safety Model	Patient Injury Model
Basis for program	1. Hospital liability theory (nonexpanded theory of hospital's duty of care; hospital responsible only for "custodial" or hotel functions). See chapter 2. 2. Historical claims experience (few claims, few dollars, claims related to "custodial" or nursing functions).	1. Changes in hospital liability theory (expanded theory of hospital's duty of care; hospital responsible for acts of medical staff, ensuring the quality of care). See chapter 2. 2. Recent claims experience (hospital is sued when physician is sued, rapid increases in claims filed, high dollar settlements).
Major source of impetus for implementing program	1. Vague, although some risk management function required by insurance carriers or alternatives.	1. The design and results of the California Medical Insurance Feasibility Study, one purpose of which was to identify the incidence of patient "potentially compensable events."
Definition of risk management	1. ". . . the identification, analysis, and evaluation of risks and the selection of the most advantageous method for treating it. . . ." A risk management program should be a totally integrated program, including employee safety, patient safety, visitor safety,	1. Risk management is the identification, analysis, evaluation, and elimination or reduction to the extent of possible risks to hospital patients, visitors, or employees. A risk management program should be a totally integrated program involving hospital

and medical staff quality assurance activities, hospital safety and security activities, a patient relations (feedback) program, and a mechanism for handling incidents, claims, and other insurance and litigation-related tasks. Adapted from "The Board's Role in Risk Management," *Trustee*, Sept. 1979, pp. 55-62; and policy statements of the Chicago Hospital Risk Pooling Program.

1. Integration/coordination of results of hospital surveillance of quality of care, safety, and patient feedback.
2. Administrative support (committees, "risk managers," and their authority) varies with each hospital's current organizational effectiveness.
3. Incident reporting procedure that includes (emphasizes) medical incidents, as opposed to "custodial."
4. Requires active physician involvement.

fire safety—in other words, a total-process safety program."—Federation of American Hospitals Malpractice Subcommittee, 1977.

Program characteristics

1. Hospital risk management (safety) committee.
2. Risk manager (safety director).
3. Incident reporting procedure.
4. Hospitalwide and departmental safety and security program, including inspections.

*Adapted, with permission, from Dixon, "Incident Reports," 1980.

potential areas of risk and to help indicate when actual risk reduction is occurring. Active communication between the risk management and quality assurance functions will improve the effectiveness of both. Lastly, the patient injury model mandates active medical staff involvement in risk management activities, a characteristic absent from the safety model.

Dixon (1980a) contends that the safety model of risk management is inappropriate to the needs of hospitals and is ineffective in preventing malpractice or malpractice loss because it bypasses meaningful involvement of physicians and the medical staff in risk management. The patient injury model is viewed as more appropriate to the needs of the hospital and more effective in preventing malpractice and malpractice loss. A conceptual strength of the patient injury model, that it requires physician leadership and medical staff participation, may also be a primary practical weakness. If the hospital relies upon active physician participation in the risk management function but is unable to obtain and maintain that participation and commitment, even a well-intentioned risk management program may be no more than an ineffective empty shell. It is important to bear in mind that there are still no proven risk management systems or models. Each hospital is responsible for tailoring risk management models and techniques to best fit its own individual characteristics.

The Tool of Incident Reporting

Every hospital risk management system, regardless of the model or philosophy upon which it is based, must have mechanisms that identify actual problems or potential risk circumstances that must be eliminated or reduced to prevent patient injury. Additionally, these mechanisms should detect and identify instances of patient injury that have already occurred. This mechanism generally takes the form of incident reporting; an incident report is usually a written description of a patient injury, adverse outcome, or untoward event.

Incident reporting has several additional purposes, although these are not always recognized or achieved. Several organizations report that the universal concept of incident reporting often becomes mired in such confusions as who should initiate an incident report, under what circumstances it should be initiated, what information it should contain, and to whom it should go. Much of this operational confusion may be the result of a general lack of understanding of the purposes of the incident report (*Amer. College of Surgeons et al.*, 1978). The *Patient Safety Manual* of the American College of Surgeons (1979) identifies four generic purposes of incident reporting:

1. An early detection system for problems and compensable incidents

2. A foundation for an early investigation of all potentially serious incidents
3. A data base for long-range problem detection, analysis, and correction
4. A cross reference with other risk detection systems

The current concept of an incident has a variety of definitions. For example, the American Hospital Association defines an incident as "any happening which is not consistent with the routine care of a particular patient" (Schwegel, 1979). Brook and Williams (1978) define the term as "any deviation from expected outcomes."

The Lovelace Medical Center defines an incident as "any happening, with or without injury, involving patient mishap or serious expression of dissatisfaction. It is a result of a patient's (or a patient's relative's or companion's) perceiving, rightly or wrongly, that the patient has in some manner been slighted, neglected, mistreated or injured" (Meyer and Wendorf, "Risk Control," 1979). Examples cited by this facility are:

- Sudden death
- Injury secondary to a procedure (a broken tooth, pressure sore from a cast, an x-ray burn)
- Drug error or reaction
- Fall
- Mishaps due to faulty equipment (such as a broken wheelchair)
- Dissatisfaction with the care or the bill
- Complaint about delays
- Hint of legal action
- Unexplained request from an attorney for a medical record

Greeley (1979) defines an incident as "any occurrence, accident or event that is not consistent with normal patient care that either did or could directly result in an injury to a patient, employee, or visitor."

In comparison with the above, past hospital policy definitions of an incident were too unspecified. Dixon (1980b) states that the past general conception of an incident encompassed "any unusual occurrence, anything out of the ordinary, or any departure from routine operation of the hospital." This vague definition elicited in most hospitals the voluminous reporting of such "incidents" as: patient or visitor slips and falls, lost patient property, and medication errors. Although these occurrences justify identification, they are of little use in pinpointing patient injuries or areas of risk that may generate a claim or litigation and result in large financial losses for the hospital. The CMIF Study (California Medical Assn., 1977) determined that traditional incident reporting of this kind detects no more than 10 percent of all potentially compensable events.

Similarly, Brook and Williams (1978) concluded that "current safety efforts in hospitals focus principally on improving the physical environment of the hospital and are not systematically concerned with preventing incidents to patients that result from the activities of physicians and other medical personnel." These authors recommend that "an incident be defined broadly so as to identify any deviation from commonly anticipated medical outcomes."

In addition to its lack of effective definition, traditional incident reporting was viewed as a nursing function (Amer. College of Surgeons, 1978; George, 1979), and, consequently, incidents that involved physicians or surgeons were rarely reported (Manvele, 1980). Besides these hindrances, incident reporting has often been regarded by hospital staff as a low priority function and is routinely performed without due consideration of its intended purpose (Amer. College of Surgeons, 1979).

Parameters of the Incident Report

After popularization of the results of the CMIF Study (California Medical Assn., 1977), it became evident that the parameters of the incident report should be expanded to include those areas that carry the potential for greatest harm to patients—medically related incidents. In furtherance of this, many insurance companies and insurance alternatives now require that medical or surgical incidents be reported as a condition of insurance coverage. In fact, many insurers have "reservation of rights" clauses (Amer. College of Surgeons, 1979). These clauses stipulate that should a malpractice suit be filed against a physician and hospital regarding an incident for which no incident report was made, the insurance carrier will defend the physician and hospital—but if the case is lost, the carrier may reserve the right not to pay the damages. In this event, the damages must be paid entirely by the physician and the hospital.

These variables, the results of the CMIF Study, and insurance requirements and conditions such as reservation of rights clauses have exerted influence upon hospitals to expand their definitions of "incidents" to include and emphasize medically or surgically related patient injuries or abnormal occurrences. This expanded system of incident reporting has been more successful than the traditional method of detecting patient injuries that are most likely to result in malpractice claims and litigation. Nevertheless, this present system of incident reporting, although an improvement, is not yet acceptably effective in detecting areas of risk and compensable patient injuries.

Duran (1979) participated in a study of Ohio hospitals that indicated that the current expanded system of incident reporting detected at most only 50 percent of the incidents that would later become claims.

Although this is a significant improvement over the 10 percent detection rate of the traditional method of incident reporting, it is still not sufficient for the development of a statistically valid hospitalwide data base for prediction and control of risks. In addition, a 50 percent detection rate of potentially compensable patient injuries is obviously an incomplete and unacceptable early warning system for impending claims. Duran broke the results of the Ohio study down further to indicate that:

> ... of all the injuries that occurred in patients' rooms in Ohio that resulted in claims, incident reports were previously filed for only 70 percent of the claims. ... Of all the injuries that occurred in the emergency departments in Ohio that resulted in claims, for 70 percent of the claims initiated, no incident reports had been previously filed.

Greeley (1979) contends that although the expanded system of incident reporting is more effective than the traditional method, it is still particularly weak in identifying operating room incidents, emergency department incidents, and medically related incidents in general.

Clearly, the present system of incident reporting suffers from problems that inhibit its effectiveness. The American College of Surgeons (1979) identified the most pervasive problems inherent in the present system of incident reporting.

- It is viewed as a nursing function, not an administrative system for risk identification.
- It is performed as a routine task with low priority, and follow-up is too slow.
- Many critical incidents are not reported, especially when physicians are involved.
- There are no criteria for determining which incidents are serious enough to warrant high-level attention.
- There is no system of collating data to detect patterns.
- Incident reports are incomplete or improperly done.
- Incident reports are viewed as potentially punitive.

In addition to these tangible problems with incident reporting, many hospitals are concerned with the possibility that, in their states, incident reports may be both legally discoverable and admissible as evidence against that hospital in a malpractice liability lawsuit. This issue is often conjured up by administrators and members of medical staffs as a reason not to engage in meaningful incident reporting. The argument that incident reports can be legally used against physicians and hospitals and therefore should not be completed is specious. Dixon (1980b) points out that incident reports should reproduce only information that is contained, or should be contained, in the medical record. Toward this end, a good incident report should not contain any analysis of the cause of the incident or any attribution of fault. Because medical records are discoverable, and because a complete medical record should contain objectively noted evidence of any patient injury, what possible difference could it make that incident reports may also be discoverable?

Regardless of the problems associated with incident reporting, it is important to bear in mind that a system for detecting actual instances of patient injury as well as for identifying problem areas and high-risk circumstances or procedures—that is, an effective incident reporting system—is the backbone of the functioning risk management program. To ensure the success of a hospital risk management program, Dixon (1980b) recommends that the information generated by the incident reporting system be:

- Reliable and valid
- Timely
- Easily interpreted
- Not freely distributed

In addition, the degree of thoroughness of an incident reporting system can move a risk management program from the level of the safety model to the more comprehensive protection inherent in the patient injury model. Emphasizing the need to include medically-related injuries in any incident reporting system, Ashly and Pearson (1976) have aptly summarized the importance of physician involvement in the hospital's risk management program:

> Most loss control or patient injury prevention programs for hospitals which exist today or are currently being planned do not attempt to address physician-related incidents, even though the majority of malpractice claims filed stem from physician-related causes.
>
> A great paradox, however, is that while hospitals have become increasingly responsible for the cost of malpractice claims, in part attributable to the doctrine of hospital corporate responsibility for the actions of staff physicians, it is generally felt that physicians are involved and are at least partially responsible for the majority of maloccurrences. James Ludlam, special advisor to the American Hospital Association on medical malpractice problems, has stated that hospital personnel-controllable claims, such as burns, medication errors, and blood transfusion errors, have been relatively stable during the last decade, while physician-controllable claims, such as those stemming from nerve damage, improper diagnosis, and cardiac arrests, have been rapidly increasing. Further, physicians are the most frequently named contributors to injuries.

The study by these authors finds a common deficiency in most loss control programs—the need for increased physician involvement on a loss control committee.

The final step in developing an effective loss prevention program is to ensure that the data from incident reports and the risk management system in general be combined with data regarding actual or potential patient injuries collected by the hospital's quality assurance activities.

Relationship to Quality Assurance

Briefly, *quality assurance* is the term used to describe the examination and evaluation of the patient care provided within a hospital toward the goal of continually improving the quality of that care (Orlikoff and Lanham, 1980). It would seem that quality assurance activities, especially those of the medical staff, would be malpractice prevention oriented in and of themselves. Also, it would seem that data from medical staff quality assurance activities would blend well with such risk management data as incident reports to improve the effectiveness of both systems. Unfortunately, this has been far from the case in the majority of hospitals.

Hospitals, for purposes of accreditation and reimbursement, have tended to follow the letter, rather than the spirit, of quality assurance requirements promulgated by such organizations as the Joint Commission on Accreditation of Hospitals and Professional Standards Review Organizations. Consequently, many hospitals have attempted to satisfy JCAH and PSRO quality assurance requirements by simply churning out the specified number of medical audits and medical care evaluation studies (criterion-based retrospective reviews of medical records to confirm that physician/practitioner performance conforms with a predetermined level). Although this in itself has been no easy task, the typical results of these "paper compliance" activities frequently have been of less than optimal quality and have demonstrated little improvement in the quality of patient care.

The tendency to focus primarily on medical audits has also hindered the efforts of hospitals in conducting other valuable quality assessment and assurance activities. Likewise, there has been little or no coordination between audit and other hospital quality assurance and risk management activities. This has resulted in a lack of needed communication, duplication of effort, cost inefficiency, and questionable (perhaps even negative) impact upon the quality of patient care (Orlikoff and Lanham, 1980). Consequently, medical staff quality assurance activities have not often contributed meaningfully toward those goals shared with risk management activities.

Several major activities in which hospitals have engaged to prevent patient injury and control malpractice claims loss have been reviewed in this chapter. Although these activities are often theoretically valid, they have not always been practically effective. The following chapter demonstrates that the majority of claims of malpractice against hospitals have been related to incidents within the control of the medical staff. It is in analyzing these claims that hospitals can discover the bases for solving their own particular malpractice problems and for fashioning new systems to prevent patient injury and malpractice liability.

References

American College of Surgeons, in consultation with the Maryland Hospital Education Institute. *Patient Safety Manual: A Guide for Establishing a Patient Safety System in Your Hospital.* Chicago: ACS, 1979.

American College of Surgeons. *Who Is Responsible for Patient Safety in Your Hospital? A report of a pilot project by the American College of Surgeons in consultation with the Maryland Hospital Education Institute.* Chicago ACS, 1978.

American College of Surgeons, American Hospital Association, and American Medical Association. *Sharing Responsibility for Patient Safety.* A report based on an Invitational Conference on Quality Care and Patient Safety, May 10-12, 1978, Chicago. Chicago: ACS, AHA, AMA, 1978.

Ashly, G.L., and Pearson, S.B. *A Study of Hospital Injury Prevention Programs* (Report G-97). Springfield, VA: National Technical Information Service, U.S. Dept. of Commerce, Nov. 29, 1976.

Brook, R.H., and Williams, K. N. Malpractice and the quality of care. *Ann. Intern. Med.* 88:836. 1978.

Brown Jr, B.L. *Risk Management for Hospitals: A Practical Approach.* Germantown, MD. Aspen Systems Corporation, 1979.

California Medical Association. *Report on the Medical Insurance Feasibility Study.* San Francisco: CMA, 1977.

Dixon, N. Conventional risk management systems and what's wrong with them. Presented at the University of Minnesota continuing medical education program: *Primum Non Nocere,* Minneapolis, Mar. 28-29, 1980a.

Dixon, N. Incident Reports. Presented at the University of Minnesota continuing medical education program *Primum Non Nocere;* Minneapolis, Mar. 28-29, 1980b.

Duran, G. Positive use of incident reports. *Hospitals.* 53:14, July 16, 1979.

George, J.E. Incident reporting. *J. Emerg. Nurs.,* 5:34, July-Aug., 1979.

Greeley, H.P. General introduction to professional liability control. Speech presented at Chicago Hospital Risk Pooling Program, 1979.

Kucera, W.R., and Ator, N. Risk management: five alternatives to commercial insurance. *Hosp. Financ. Manage.* 32:10, Oct. 1978.

Manuele, F.A. Physicians as partners in patient safety in hospitals. Presented at the American Medical Association seminar, "Medical Staff: Physician, Friend or Foe," Chicago, Apr. 24, 1980.

Mehr, R.I., and Hedges, B.A. *Risk Management in the Business Enerprise.* Homewood, IL: Richard D. Irwin, Inc., 1963.

Meyer, N.H., and Wendorf, B. Risk control: from management of crises to prevention of incidents. *Qual. Rev. Bull.,* 5:27, 1979.

Orlikoff, J.E., and Lanham. G.B. Quality assurance and risk management: learning to live together. *J. Qual. Assurance* 2:8, 1980.

Schwegel, K. Physicians join in efforts to reduce risks. *The Hosp. Med. Staff.* 8:11, Nov. 1979.

Tanenbaum, J., and Korsak, A. Commercial carriers still dominate insurance coverage. *Hospitals.* 52:48, Sept. 1, 1978.

CHAPTER 5

Physician-Related Medical Injury

The preceding chapters have differentiated between custodial negligence, which is the domain of "slips and falls" addressed by the traditional administratively directed risk management program, and professional negligence, which is the domain of medically related patient injury, and which must be addressed by a physician-directed program of prevention. The purpose of this chapter is to identify the specific targets of previous malpractice claims in the latter area and to explore the various steps that can be taken to respond to the aspect of malpractice that concerns medically related patient injury.

ANALYZING THE EVIDENCE OF MOST FREQUENT INJURIES

Nature of the Problem

There have been numerous and varying attempts to describe or classify the malpractice problem. For example, a study of 10,000 claims closed in 1974 disclosed that three-fourths were against physicians; of these, 81 percent arose from treatment of patients in hospitals and 16 percent arose from incidents in a physician's office (*Parthenon*, 1979). Not only have suits been related to hospital care, but also they have most often singled out surgery and postsurgical care. Brook and Williams (1978) report that of all indemnity dollars, 84 percent are for hospital-related claims and 82 percent relate to surgery and surgical care.

As to the site within the hospital where a potentially compensable event occurs, the California Medical Association (1977) lists the following:

Operating room	71.8%
Patient's room	12.0%

Radiology department	5.8%
Labor and delivery area	4.6%
Emergency department	2.6%
Unknown or other	2.1%
Nursery	0.7%
Critical care units	0.4%
	100.0%

The same study classifies potentially compensable events by causal factors and listed these, in order of frequency:

Specific procedures	66.1%
Drugs and biologics	18.8%
Devices	4.1%
Nondiagnosis	2.6%
General medical management	2.6%
Misdiagnosis	2.2%
Anesthesia management	2.0%
Nursing management	1.6%
	100.0%

A study by the American Medical Association General Council considered 2,193 malpractice suits from April 1, 1971, to March 1, 1978. The 877 cases that involved hospitals were classified in the following manner:

Negligence in observation or management	396
Falls	240
Emergency department incidents	190
All other	51

Curran (1979) points out that a shift has occurred in the target of the plaintiff's allegations over the past decade: The HEW Secretary's Commission reported that in 1970, 86 percent of claims alleged improper treatment and only 14 percent improper diagnosis. The later Saint Paul survey of claims (1973-78) found 50 percent alleging improper therapy and an increase to 25 percent in allegations of improper diagnosis. This trend away from "sins of commission" toward "sins of omission" was accompanied by a shift away from res ipsa loquitor allegations toward the derivative hospital liability because of an extended duty of care.

The Ohio Joint Underwriting Authority analyzed claims from 150 hospitals in its state and classified them in the following order of frequency (Mikolaj, 1978):

Negligence in the surgical suite (including anesthesia)	11.0%
Improper diagnosis	10.1%
Medical errors	9.2%
Lack of staff attention	9.2%

Hospital bed and table falls	9.2%
Accidents unrelated to treatment	6.9%
Burns (all)	4.3%
Infection	4.1%
Lost personal property	3.1%
All other combined	32.1%

Injury from Medical Devices

Some authors have studied certain aspects of the problem in greater detail. Morris (1979) has analyzed liability arising from the use of medical devices and has provided valuable insight about a widespread problem: some 1,100 companies produce 12,000 different types of biomedical devices, with total annual retail sales of $5 billion! Examples of such devices in common hospital use are anesthesia machines, respirators, x-ray machines, computed tomography scanners, electroencephalographs, cardiac defibrillators, and electronic monitors. A National Association of Insurance Commissioners tabulation of 16,592 malpractice claims closed from July 1976 to June 1978 reports equipment-related injury 711 times in the 6,317 incidents identified. Morris estimates there were 10,000 such injuries between 1960 and 1970, causing 731 deaths, 512 of which were due to defective heart valves alone. The Parthenon Insurance Company (1979) reports that, of all "preventable" anesthesia mishaps, 82 percent are due to human error and 14 percent to equipment failure.

Injury from Infections

Other authors have studied nosocomial (hospital-acquired) infections as a part of the problem. The overall evidence of nosocomial infections in acute general (short-stay) hospitals is approximately 5 percent, according to the Center for Disease Control. This rate produces 1.5 million infections annually that result in or contribute to 15,000 deaths at an annual cost of $1 billion (Missouri Professional Liability Insurance Assn., 1978).

Stamm (1979) claims that 45 percent of all nosocomial infections (or more than 850,000 per year) may be related to the patient's exposure to "medical devices," the most common of which is the urinary catheter. Other common devices include intravascular monitors, respiratory therapy or anesthesia equipment, or intravenous infusion devices. More specialized devices include orthopedic or cardiac prostheses and hemodialysis shunts.

Rhame's (1979) analysis of nosocomial infections concluded that 40 percent of such events were urinary tract infections; of these, two-thirds occurred in conjunction with urinary catheters. Next in frequency were surgical wound infections, which accounted for an additional 25 percent of nosocomial infections, followed by pneumonia.

The California Medical Insurance Feasibility (CMIF) Study (1977) also emphasized the frequency of postprocedural infections, which were the largest category within their "adverse effects of treatment" group.

Finally, Polk and Finn (1979) conclude that "post-operative infection . . . remains the most frequently encountered complication of surgical therapy, occurring in 4 to 7 percent of all surgical cases." (The Impact of Infections . . . 1978).

Injury from Medication Administration and Errors

Another area of hospital liability that has been analyzed is that of medication errors, the frequency of which depends on the definition of an "error" (Missouri Professional Liability Insurance Assn., 1978). These errors occur most commonly on the day shift or evening shift and most frequently involve the wrong dose of medication. Other common errors are administration to the wrong patient, administration of the wrong medication, and the omission of a dose, all of which are potentially serious and preventable.

The CMIF Study reported "drugs and biologics" as a frequent (19 percent of all) cause of potentially compensable events and found at 10 categories caused 65 percent of all drug-related potentially compensable events. These agents were:

1. Estrogens/progestins
2. Anticoagulants
3. Adrenocorticoids
4. Aspirin
5. Tranquilizers
6. Blood transfusions
7. Digitalis and cogeners
8. Antidiabetic agents
9. Antihypertensive agents
10. Tetracycline

Finally, the Saint Paul Companies analyzed 21,872 claims during the period from October 1973 to December 1977 to determine the 12 most frequent allegations (2) of malpractice. The results are shown in table 3, opposite.

Physicians Most Vulnerable to Suits

Incidents, or adverse patient occurrences, are not distributed evenly among all physicians. Although the N.A.I.C. data referred to previously (*Amer. Medical News*, 1978) indicated a 4.5 percent incidence of

TABLE 3
The 12 Most Frequent Claims of Malpractice*

Allegation	Number of Claims	
A. Improper treatment		
1. Surgical error	1,747	
2. Lack of supervision/control	809	
3. Fracture or dislocation	712	
4. Birth-related problems	648	
5. Surgical, postoperative	623	
6. Surgical, improper procedure	607	
7. Drug side effect	579	
8. Infection	544	
		6,269
B. Failure to diagnose		
9. Fracture or dislocation	803	
10. Cancer	552	
		1,355
C. Surgery		
11. Postoperative complications	650	
12. Lack of informed consent	442	
		1,092
Total	8,716	

* Based on analysis of 21,872 claims made against the St. Paul Company between October 1973 and December 1977. This table originally appeared in the "Impact" section of *American Medical News*, April 28, 1978. Reprinted with permission.

closed claims against physicians involved in patient care in 1975, the surgical specialties, as table 3 suggests, are more vulnerable to claims; orthopedists, obstetricians or gynecologists practicing surgery, plastic surgeons, head and neck surgeons, cardiovascular surgeons, and neurosurgeons are at greatest risk. In fact, 70 percent of NAIC cases (2,961 of 4,284) involved surgical error.

On the basis of such findings, physicians are often divided into "classes" by the insurance industry in order to enhance actuarial predictions and relate premium structure to claims experience. Table 4, page 48, presents such a classification along with the number of claims experienced, by specialty.

An American Medical Association survey (*Amer. Medical News*, 1978) also disclosed a significant difference in physician experience in

TABLE 4
Frequency of Malpractice Suits by Insurance Category*

Class	Specialty in Class	Number of Claims
I	General practice/family practice	679
II	General practice doing minor surgery	472
III	General practice doing major surgery	711
IV	General surgery/urology	496
V	General surgery	1,284
VI	Obstetrics/gynecology	287
VII	Orthopedic surgery	243

* When claims are categorized, the frequency of claims shown here is not as important to insurance companies as the severity of the patient injury. Thus, even though Class III physicians (those in general practice doing surgery) may generate more claims than Class VII physicians (those doing orthopedic surgery), the claims generated by the Class VII physicians will tend to reflect more serious patient injuries and therefore result in larger financial losses to the insurance company.

various geographic regions of the United States. In the three years prior to the survey, physicians in the East South-Central states had a 23 percent rate of suits, followed closely by a 22.2 percent rate in the Mountain states, a 17.5 percent rate in the middle Atlantic area, and only 15.9 percent in the Pacific states. An age breakdown indicates that the age group 49-65 reports a higher incidence (18.9 percent) of suits than do physicians in other age brackets. The same survey indicates that the 21.9 percent rate of suits reported by all surgeons is exceeded only by the anesthesiologists, who reported a rate of 28.6 percent over the three-year period of the survey.

Schwartz and Komesar (1978) report a marked small area variation in the frequency of claims, noting that in a four-year period in Los Angeles, 46 physicians (0.6 percent of the 8,000 physicians in the area) accounted for 10 percent of all claims and 30 percent of all payments by one insurance plan.

Translating Claims Data into a Loss Prevention Program

These kinds of data have only limited use in planning a hospital-based program to prevent physician-related injury. Such an effort must be based on a more careful breakdown of the claims data, as has been done by Tancredi's study (1974) of 350 orthopedic cases from the period 1910 to 1972. First, he divided the cases into anatomic or procedural categories.

When a fracture was the clinical situation that led to a suit, the site of fracture was (in alphabetic order, some classified more than once):

Ankle	18
Arm or forearm	53
Elbow	13
Finger	3
Foot or toe	6
Hip	15
Knee	3
Leg or thigh	88
Shoulder girdle	3
Skull and jaw	16
Vertebrae	15
Wrist	9
Compound	11

These data would be more useful, or course, if they were accompanied by a report of the frequency with which each type of fracture was initially presented for treatment. Although physician-readers can generally infer the relative frequency of these fractures from experience, the absence of denominator data limits the usefulness of the analysis for the individual hospital in planning its prevention program. Tancredi (1974) also created a classification of causes of 117 "medically avoidable" cases (some classified in more than one way) as follows:

Diagnosis-related cases

Error in diagnosis	3
Delay in diagnosis	2
Failure to diagnose	4
Improper measures of diagnosis	17
Failure to recognize need to alter diagnosis	7

Treatment-related cases

Inappropriate treatment (includes unusual or unique procedure, not referring patient to a specialist, and incomplete treatment)	13
Delay in treatment	21
Failure to treat	3
Lack of implementing skills	
Nonsurgical, that is, casts	26
Surgical	4

Need to modify treatment	8
Secondary injury	
Foreign body	6
Other	9
Informed consent	2
Treatment error	7
Follow-up-related cases	
Inadequate follow-up	6
Abandonment	2

After identifying adverse medical events that are highly avoidable, Tancredi noted two areas that could be easily prevented but that occurred most frequently: (1) adverse outcomes from failure or delay in diagnosing and treatment (including not ordering X rays) and (2) Volkmann's contracture and/or bandages.

King (1978) also developed a list of medically related patient injuries that are the most frequent reasons for claims:

- Death and/or brain damage during anesthesia for all types of surgery
- Death due to failure to diagnose cancer
- Death due to failure to diagnose and treat adequately underlying coronary pathologic conditions
- Reaction to diagnostic procedures and dyes (aortagrams, intravenous pyelograms, and so forth)
- Postoperative infection
- Laparoscopy
- All obstetric and gynecological procedures

Developing a Classification System

Tancredi's results and a list like the one King presented provide a sound basis for developing a rational and useful classification system, which is essential in establishing an effective program of physician-related patient injury prevention. Because detection and prevention of such injuries is not being accomplished by current risk management programs that emphasize traditional incident reporting, it seems clear that we must define an incident to include the things physicians do. The work of Tancredi and King suggests answers to such questions as the following: What are physician incidents? Who reports them and to whom? What is the severity threshold to initiate action? Is the elective removal of the uterus with nominal or no pathology an incident, for example? "Unnecessary" surgery, as such, rarely leads to a malpractice claim (Schwartz and Komesar, 1978).

Fainter (1979) has suggested adding two generic criteria to every audit performed in the hospital: (1) any hospital-incurred trauma, and (2) any readmission within 30, 60, or 90 days. Variations from the latter criterion (which would have a zero percent standard) could be easily detected by a surveillance system. The former, however, requires a system for capture of data. The concept of "trauma" needs a working definition and a threshold level established. Fainter suggests that it be defined by "incident reports," which again places the burden on a different type of incident report from the traditional one.

An exception review approach to medical care evaluation that goes beyond Fainter's attempt to reorient the incident reporting concept has been suggested. It suggests review of:

- All records requested by an attorney
- All deaths in patients less than 50 years of age
- All readmissions
- All reoperations
- All emergency department activities
- Toxic drugs

Some of these areas have been studied by other authors. Dodge (1979) recommends an emergency department surveillance program that focuses on problems known to be associated with risk of lawsuit:

- The hospital's legal duty to provide emergency care should be defined, with clear procedures for triage, transfer of cases that exceed the capabilities of the hospital, definition of duty of care between the hospital's own emergency department staff and the attending staff, and so forth.
- Problems with alcoholic patients should be anticipated and clear policies and procedures developed for dealing with evaluation, informed consent, failure of patient compliance, coping with combative behavior, and so forth.
- The emergency department record should be defined as to data required, timeliness, and storage and retrieval and should be coordinated with the inpatient and outpatient records into a unit record that supports care continuity.
- Communication breakdowns should be anticipated and circumvented to the degree possible by clear and effective procedures for prompt notification of the attending physician, division of authority and responsibility between the emergency department on-call staff and the attending staff, and patient instruction to enhance follow-up and compliance with treatment plans.

Dodge quotes the DHEW Secretary's Medical Malpractice Commission report (1973), which concludes that 12 percent of all hospital claims originated in the emergency department. Since the data collected in the early '70s, patient encounters in hospital emergency departments have steadily increased, making one suspect emergency care to be more important than ever as a focus of activities to prevent patient injury and suit.

Craddick (1979) has described a system to detect and prevent medically related patient injury that is designed to be comprehensive and concurrent. Called the "Medical Management Analysis" (MMA) system, it is subtitled "a professional liability warning mechanism." Craddick built on her experience with the CMIF study to modify the generic criteria used in that effort into the patient safety screening criteria shown in table 5, page 53. Craddick recommends adding review components for tissue (surgical case review), transfusions, antibiotics, and medical records to the criteria set to produce a comprehensive review mechanism; her work includes an implementation model describing the steps in the system.

Greeley, recognizing the concentration of physician- related liability in the surgical care area, has developed a surgical monitoring system with these components:
- Tissue (surgical case) review
- Transfusion review
- Mortality review
- Morbidity conference
- Surgical audit
- Infection review
- Antibiotic review
- Medical record review
- Proctoring all new physicans
- Recredentialing

This system, which uses generic criteria to screen surgical care records monthly, is described in more detail in chapter 6.

Greeley's system is noteworthy for its inclusion of credentialing as a component of a comprehensive system designed to prevent physician-related adverse patient occurrences. Credentialing, as used in the context of the hospital medical staff, refers to the process by which medical staff appointments and clinical privileges are determined initially and recurrently, the latter referred to as "reappraisal." This activity, mandated by the Joint Commission on Accreditation of Hospitals (1980), can be a potent component of a comprehensive patient protection system; indeed, recruitment and retention of highly competent practitioners may be the keystone of such a system. Unfortunately, credentialing has often been a *pro forma* activity in a hospital, principally because the reappraisal process has not utilized data derived from evaluation of practitioner performance in the recredentialing decision.

TABLE 5
Patient Safety Screening Criteria*

Criterion	Exceptions
First Priority	
1. Admission for adverse results of outpatient management in the hospital's outpatient department, emergency department, or private office of a member of the medical staff (for example, delayed diagnosis, conditions attributed to outpatient drug therapy, or complications from office procedures)	1. None
2. Admission for a complication resulting from incomplete management on a previous hospital admission	2. Readmission for chronic conditions with follow-up documented on discharge summary and no indication of mismanagement
3. Hospital-incurred trauma (for example, patient accidents, procedural errors, shocks and burns)	3. None
4. Adverse reactions to medications, transfusions, and anesthetics	4. None
5. Transfer from general care to a special care unit	5. Planned transfer or intensive care unit used as a recovery room
6. Patient returned to operating room on same admission	6. Planned return
7. Operation for perforation, laceration, or tear or injury incurred during an invasive procedure (for example, repair of injury received during intubations, catheterizations, invasive x-ray procedures, endoscopies, percutaneous aspirations, and percutaneous biopsies)	7. None
8. Cancellation of or repeat diagnostic procedure because of improper preparation of patient, technician error, or equipment failure	8. None

* Reprinted, with permission, of Joyce W. Craddick, M.D., and the American College of Surgeons, from *Patient Safety Manual,* 1979.

TABLE 5 (cont.)

Criterion	Exceptions
First Priority (cont.)	
9. Unplanned removal of an organ or part of an organ during an operative procedure	9. None
10. Other complications and unexplained major diagnostic and therapeutic maneuvers	10. None
11. Myocardial infarction during or within 48 hours of surgical procedure	11. Preoperative workup included normal electrocardiogram and enzymes and no cardiac history; emergency operative procedure
12. Cardiac or respiratory arrest	12. None
13. Length of stay exceeds number of days listed at 90th percentile	13. Stay due to nonmedical problems (awaiting transfer to long-term care facility)
14. Death	14. None
15. Patient or family threatens suit	15. None
Second Priority	
1. Transfer to another acute care facility	1. Mandatory transfer for administrative reasons; transfer for a test or procedure not available at this hospital
2. Infection not present on admission (nosocomial)	2. None
3. Neurological deficit present on discharge, not present on admission	3. None
4. Febrile on last full day prior to or day of discharge	4. None

TABLE 5 (cont.)

Criterion	Exceptions
Second Priority (cont.)	
5. Parenteral analgesics on last full day prior to or day of discharge	5. Terminal cancer, preoperative medication, postoperative medication for 48 hours subsequent to operative procedure
6. Patient leaves before discharge authorized	6. None
7. Patient refuses to pay all or part of bill	7. None
8. Claim, call, letter, or papers received	8. None

The standard is quite specific in its expectations: "The chief of the department . . . should contribute information in writing relative to the individual's professional performance, judgment, and when appropriate, technical skill, and should indicate any effect thereon of the staff member's health status." It states further, "other reappraisal parameters should include . . . patterns of care as demonstrated by reviews conducted by committees, such as utilization review, infection control, tissue, medical record, pharmacy/therapeutics, and patient care evaluation."

It is interesting to note the requirement that each physician's health status be considered in the reappraisal process. There is good reason to posit that much patient harm and potential hospital liability are related to the bigger problem of "the sick physician." Under euphemisms such as "disabled physician" and "impaired physician," both state statutes and professional associations are beginning to recognize and deal with the problems of superannuation, alcoholism, chemical dependency, and emotional disorders among physicians. Such activities may prevent patient injuries and rehabilitate sick physicians while avoiding liability for both physicians and hospitals.

One of the "captive" insurance programs described in chapter 4, the Hospital Underwriters Mutual (HUM) of New York (1978), has developed surveillance systems that focus on the areas of greatest potential for patient injury (anesthesia, emergency department, operating room, special care unit, and so forth). The program conducts a monthly surgical case review that cross-indexes the variations from its screening criteria by surgeon, to provide data input to the reappraisal process. The HUM system also includes a well designed incident report form that permits data entry into a computerized information system capable of spotting patterns and problems. The HUM "Early Warning Alert System" criteria are very much like those developed by Craddick in that they are generic and comprehensive. These criteria require review of the following situations:

- Prior hospitalization within one year
- Apgar score of 4 or less
- Hospital-incurred trauma
- Adverse drug reactions
- Transfer to isolation, intensive care unit, cardiac care unit
- Transfer to another acute care facility
- Return to surgical suite
- Repair of punctured organ, and so forth
- Unplanned removal of organ, and so forth
- Wound infection
- Neurologic deficit
- Length of stay greater than 90th percentile for diagnosis
- Cardiac or respiratory arrest
- Fever on discharge
- Discharge of newborn weighing less than 5 pounds (2,250 grams)
- Return for emergency care within 48 hours after emergency or outpatient treatment

Review of this list indicates that thoughtful efforts are under way to prevent patient injury and professional liability.

Fifer (1979) has contributed to these efforts with a list of activities that he believes would comprehensively address the area of physician-related patient injuries:

- The physician-related incident must be defined operationally.
- Severity thresholds must be established for physician-related incidents.
- Early detection of the "impaired physician" must be accomplished.
- "Scrub-ins" (analogous to "check rides" for pilots) must be implemented for high-risk procedures.
- Second opinions must be invoked prior to elective surgery for high-risk procedures.
- Computerized feedback systems of the type described by McDonald (1976) must be designed to prevent oversight of abnormal laboratory values, x-ray reports, and so forth.
- Surveillance of high-risk procedures should include laparoscopy, pacemaker insertion, radiotherapy, hip replacement

plastic surgery, and fracture of dislocation X rays.
- Informed consent procedures must be designed and monitored.
- Patient complaints must be aggregated for pattern analysis.
- Discharges against medical advice (elopements) must be reviewed immediately.
- Lawsuits against physicians must be identified and tracked.
- Deaths must be reviewed systematically and effectively.
- Unimproved or complicated cases must be reviewed in the individual and the aggregate dimensions.
- Readmissions must be reviewed.
- A hospitalwide program to reduce medication errors must be implemented.
- A drug utilization review program must be implemented.

The contribution of "toxic drug" use to the incidence of patient injury has also been explored by several authors.

Monitoring Drug Use

An earlier section in this chapter mentions the 10 categories of drugs or biologics most frequently associated with potentially compensable events, according to the CMIF study; one of these was tetracycline, an antibiotic. Caldwell and Cluff (1974) put the likelihood of adverse reactions to antibiotics commonly used in the hospital in a significant range (see also Kunin and Sabatino, 1979). Gentamycin carries a 7.7 percent reaction rate; penicillinase-resistant penicillins (other than methicillin), 7.3 percent; ampicillin, 5.7 percent; and the cephalosporins, 5.2 percent. These are potent antibiotics that are often used to combat serious, even life-threatening, infectious diseases and complications.

In those situations, adverse reaction rates of 5 to 8 percent might be justified as clinically acceptable and the liability potential associated with such reactions as inevitable and even justified by the good they do. The fact is, however, that much antibiotic use in hospitals has been described as "irrational." Achong and colleagues at McMaster University (1977a) focused on the parenteral use of potent and potentially toxic antibiotics. They found that 12.9 percent of 219 patients admitted during a three-month period received at least one of four parenteral antibiotics (gentamycin, cloxacillin, ampicillin, and cephalothin). They concluded (1977b) that therapy was "irrational" in 42 percent of the surgical cases, 50 percent of the gynecological cases, and 12 percent of the medical cases.

Roberts and Visconti (1972) had earlier reached much the same conclusion, reporting that 65.6 percent of all antibiotic therapy was irrational.

Kunin and coauthors (1973) concluded that 57.5 percent of patients in a major teaching hospital received either an inappropriate antibiotic or an inappropriate dose. Hospital antibiotic therapy is only one example of physician activities that have the potential to injure patients, but whose injury potential can be reduced by invoking surveillance and control methods. Such methods are usually established in response to hospital accreditation standards that require hospital medical staffs to monitor antibiotic use as part of the pharmacy and therapeutics function of drug utilization review (Joint Commission on Accreditation of Hospitals, 1980).

Another related concern is the inappropriate use of psychoactive drugs, singly and in combinations. A large Veterans Administration hospital that analyzed its "slip and fall" incidents found that polypharmacy with psychoactive drugs frequently preceded these incidents (Warner, 1978). Other authors have concluded that psychoactive drugs can produce adverse reactions, especially in the elderly (Learoyd, 1972). Achong and coauthors (1978) surveyed 1,431 patients over age 65 and found that 24.9 percent received one psychoactive drug and that 26.6 percent had received two or three drugs simultaneously. They conclude, with other authors, that a program to monitor use and control inappropriate use of these drugs must involve physicians if behavioral change is to occur. A committee of the American Psychiatric Association has recently published a set of criteria to be used for review and control of psychoactive drug utilization (Dorsey and others, 1979). If used as an ongoing monitor or control system rather than a one-time audit "study," such review has the potential to prevent the inappropriate use of psychoactive drugs that are implicated in so many hospital falls.

In addition to criteria for antibiotic (*Quality Review Bulletin*, 1979) and psychoactive drug therapy, criteria are available that will enable a hospital medical staff to review the use of blood (*Quality Review Bulletin*, 1977) and medications known to be associated with a high rate of misuse, toxicity, and claims, such as warfarin and digoxin (Keys, 1979).

These recommendations for monitoring drug use—as well as the earlier section of this chapter on developing generic criteria for identifying potentially compensable incidents—are, of course, prescriptive in the extreme. Few hospitals can begin to cope with the content of such a comprehensive program, to say nothing about its organization and data requirements. To assist hospitals in initiating plans for a comprehensive loss prevention program, the following three chapters describe in greater detail how some of the above recommendations can be implemented through new programs and how current hospital efforts in risk management and quality assurance can be improved.

References

Achong, M.R., and others. Prescribing the psychoactive drugs for chronically ill elderly patients. *CMA J.* 118:1503, 1978.

_____. Rational and irrational use of antibiotics in a Canadian teaching hospital. *CMA J.* 116:256, 1977a.

_____. Changes in hospital antibiotic therapy after a quality-of-use study. *Lancet.* 2:1118, Nov. 26, 1977b.

Amer. Medical News, Chicago, Apr. 28, 1978.

Brook, R.H., and Williams, K.N. Malpractice and the quality of care. *Ann. Intern. Med.* 88:836, 1978.

Caldwell, J.R., and Cluff, L.E. Adverse reactions to antimicrobial agents. *J. Amer. Med. Assoc.* 230:77, 1974.

California Medical Association. *Report on the Medical Insurance Feasibility Study.* San Francisco: CMA, 1977.

Craddick, J.W. The medical management analysis system: professional liability warning mechanism. *Qual. Rev. Bull.* 5:2, 1979.

Curran, W.J. Malpractice claims: new data and trends. *New Engl. J. Med.* 300:26, 1979.

Dodge, D.D., and others. Developing a statewide loss control program. *Qual. Rev. Bull.* 5:31, 1979.

Dorsey, R., and others. Psychopharmacological screening criteria development project. *J. Amer. Med. Assoc.* 241:1021, 1979.

Fainter, J. Audit focus: HCA hospitals add generic risk management criteria to all audits. *Audit Action Letter IV* (19), June 1979.

Fifer, W.R. Risk management and medical malpractice: an overview of the issues. *Qual. Rev. Bull.* 5:4, Apr. 1979.

_____. Risk management and quality assurance: integration for optimal effectiveness. *Qual. Rev. Bull.* 5:15, Aug. 1979.

_____. Toward an integrated approach to quality assurance/risk management activities. Foreword in *Solutions,* Chicago: Case Communications, Inc., 1979.

Hospital Underwriters Mutual Co. *Risk Management Program.* Tarrytown, NY: the Company, 1978.

The impact of infections on medical care in the U.S. *Annals of Med.* 89:737, suppl., Nov. 1978.

Keys, P.W., and Narduzzi, J.V. Drug audit: a component of quality assurance. *Qual. Rev. Bull.* 5:17, 1979.

King, T.C., and others. Symposium on malpractice. *NY State J. Med.* 78:1272, 1978.

Kunin, C.M., and others. Use of antibiotics: a brief exposition of the problem and some tentative solutions. *Ann. Intern. Med.* 79:555, 1973.

Kunin, C.M., and Sabatino, F.G. Antibiotic usage surveillance: an overview of the issues. *Qual. Rev. Bull.* 5:4-8, Jan. 1979.

Learoyd, B.M. Psychotropic drugs and the elderly patient. *Med. J. Australia* 1:1131, 1972.

McDonald, C.J. Protocol-based computer reminders, the quality of care and the nonperfectability of man. *New Engl. J. Med.* 295:1351, 1976.

Mikolaj, P.J. Hospital association determines nature of closed claims in state. *Hospitals.* 52:53, Feb. 1, 1978.

Morris, C. Defective devices—who's liable? *Hosp. Med. Staff.* 8:1, May 1979.

Missouri Professional Liability Insurance Association. *Risk Management Letter.* Jefferson City, MO: MPLIA, Dec. 1978.

Parthenon Insurance Company Newsletter. Nashville, Jan./Feb., 1979.

Polk Jr., H.C., and Finn, M. Prevention of surgical wound infection. *Qual. Rev. Bull.* 5:18, 1979.

Quality Review Bulletin Editorial Board: In another vein: rationale and criteria for studying blood transfusions. *Qual. Rev. Bull.* 3:11, 1977.

Quality Review Bulletin Special Issue: Antibiotic Review and Drug Utilization. *Qual. Rev. Bull.* 5:(1), 1979 (entire issue).

Rhame, F. *Medicine Grand Rounds.* Minneapolis: University of Minnesota Hospitals, Mar. 8, 1979.

Roberts, A.W., and Visconti, J.A. The rational and irrational use of systemic antimicrobial drugs. *Amer. J. Hosp. Pharm.* 29:828, 1972.

Schwartz, W.B., and Komesar, N.K. Doctors, damages, and deterrence—an economic view of medical malpractice. *New Engl. J. Med.* 298:1282, 1978.

Stamm, W.E. Nosocomial infections due to medical devices. *Qual. Rev. Bull.* 5:23, 1979.

Tancredi, L.J. Identifying avoidable adverse events in medicine. *Med. Care* 12:935, 1974.

Warner, A.M. personal communication, 1978.

CHAPTER 6

Mounting a Program to Prevent Medically Related Patient Injuries

Only after a medical staff has accepted the fact that its members' activities contribute significantly to the incidence of patient injury, is it likely that it will begin, as it must, to employ all reasonable methods to identify, confront, and prevent problems that may generate patient injury. The medical staff is the basic organizational unit of the hospital that is capable of effectively evaluating and controlling the practice of practitioners within the institution. This capability must logically be translated into a primary responsibility of the medical staff. The fulfillment of this responsibility, through amplification of the medical staff's collective experience, will involve the innovation and conducting of new, effective approaches to prevent medically related patient injuries and to minimize malpractice liability exposure. This responsibility will also be expressed through the modification and refinement of existing quality assurance and risk management techniques.

By modifying and improving existing activities, such as incident reporting, a hospital can significantly improve the quality of its patient injury data base, and therefore more effectively identify and resolve problems. Instituting new policies and implementing new activities are also critical to the functioning of an effective, medically directed, patient injury prevention program. By concentrating on a few fundamental principles, the medical staff can successfully identify those practitioners most likely to generate medically related patient injuries and prevent them from joining the medical staff. Additionally, the medical staff can institute effective procedures to monitor members of the staff to ensure that any practice problems will be detected and corrected before they appear as compensable patient injuries.

This chapter presents techniques and examples of how to modify existing risk management activities and how to devise and institute new activities to prevent patient injury and reduce the probability of malpractice liability.

MONITORING THE MEDICAL STAFF

Appointment of New Applicants to the Medical Staff

Every hospital's medical staff has rules and regulations that govern the process of reviewing and recommending the appointment of a new applicant to the medical staff. Unfortunately, these procedures are not always followed in a meaningful, consistent fashion and therefore may be of little value in reliably assuring the qualifications, skill, and judgment of applicants to the medical staff. By controlling who joins its ranks, the medical staff is obviously an integral component of a medically directed patient injury prevention program.

The purpose of this section is not to advocate revision of each hospital's medical staff credentialing procedure. Rather, the purpose is to encourage each hospital medical staff to review its credentialing procedure and to advocate a strict and rigorous adherence to that procedure for each new applicant. This point cannot be stressed too strongly. Discrepancies between what the appointment and credentialing procedure requires and how the process is actually conducted represent a serious breach of the medical staff's responsibility to new applicants, to itself and the hospital, and to the safety of patients.

For purposes of consideration and comparison, an example follows of a procedure used by several hospitals for appointing members to the medical staff, credentialing, and delineating clinical privileges.

In addition to ensuring that all medical or allied health professional files are maintained under lock by the medical staff secretary, the procedure to follow with new applicants is as follows:

1. Each applicant will be provided with an application form, a form for requesting clinical privileges, a copy of the hospital bylaws and fair hearing plan, and necessary supplemental information.
2. Upon receipt of a completed application, the medical staff secretary will:
   - Review and confirm that the application form is complete
   - Request any additional information needed to complete the application
   - Verify contents of the application by:
     —requesting an AMA information sheet
     —sending reference request letters to all listed references and past hospital affiliations

—contacting the state for licensure verification

—sending a form letter to past and current malpractice insurance carriers

—verifying the Bureau of Narcotics and Dangerous Drugs (BNDD) number

- Receive and file letters of reference and document any failure to receive such letters
- Send copies of unanswered letters to applicant requesting that they be completed
- Prepare a list of telephone contacts for the vice-president of professional services (or equivalent)
- Assist the vice-president for professional services in preparing an administrative review for the credentials committee

3. Schedule the new applicant to attend the first credentials committee meeting after the application records have been completed, generally within one month from the date of receipt of an application.

4. Forward the completed credentials file and clinical privileges requested to the appropriate department chairman prior to review by the credentials committee.

5. Forward the recommendation of the credentials committee to the executive committee.

6. Prepare one of two form letters for the administrator's signature, after executive committee action.

7. Prepare final letter for applicant, once board has taken final action.

Several of the forms used to complete the above procedure are included here: figure 4, page 79, is a form letter request for reference; figure 5, page 80, is a questionnaire to be completed as part of the reference; and figure 6, page 81, is a form to monitor the application review process.

Observation of New Appointees to the Medical Staff

Every hospital's medical staff should have a provision in its bylaws requiring that new appointees to the staff serve a period of observation or probation prior to the granting of full nonproctored privileges. A provision worded as follows would serve this function.

Except as otherwise determined by the board, all initial appointments to any category of the staff shall be subject to a period of observation of six months. Each appointee shall be assigned initially to a department where his or her performance shall be observed by the chairman of the department or such chairman's designee. The purpose of this observation is to determine the appointee's eligibility for continued staff membership in the staff category to which he or she was initially appointed and for exercising the clinical privileges initially granted in that department. His or her exercise of clinical privileges in any other department shall also be subject to observation by that department's chairman or his or her designee. An initial appointee shall remain subject to observation until he or she has furnished to the credentials commitee (or the medical executive committee) and to the chief executive officer a statement signed by the chairman of the department to which he or she is assigned. This statement should verify that the appointee meets all of the qualifications, has discharged all of the responsibilities, and has not exceeded or abused the prerogatives of the staff category to which he or she is appointed. The committee must also receive a statement signed by the chairman of the departments in which the appointee will exercise clinical privileges that he or she has satisfactorily demonstrated his or her ability to exercise the clinical privileges initially granted to him or her.

This period of observation enables a medical staff to carefully evaluate the qualifications and the medical and surgical skills and judgment of new staff appointees. In the past, mechanisms used by hospitals to perform this function ranged from a perfunctory announcement that the period of observation has passed to a systematically documented evaluation of the new appointee in relation to clinical competence and adherence to basic medical staff rules.

The thrust of the provision for a period of observation is clear. All new applicants to a medical staff should bear the responsibility of demonstrating to their colleagues that they are competent and capable of providing patient care consistent with the standards set by the particular institution. At a minimum, every new applicant should be reviewed using one of the following two systems: (1) personal proctoring of new physicians, or (2) retrospective review (medical care evaluation) of the quality of care provided by the new medical staff member.

Personal proctoring of new physicians

The rules and regulations of some hospitals currently require that new members to the medical staff be personally proctored in each field by other staff physicians with complete privileges in that particular field. It is important in the application of this type of a proctoring system to ensure accurate documentation of the process and results of the proctoring experience. Figure 7, page 82, and figure 8, page 83, illustrate a type of surgical proctoring system that is in use at a number of hospitals.

This system generates a certain amount of information on all physicians joining the medical staff, and it also requires that they present specified information to the surgical committee at the end of their first six months of practice at the hospital. At that time, the surgical committee reviews the surgical proctoring reports and performs an aggregate analysis of the number and type of surgical cases performed by a newly appointed physician. In the event that the number of surgical procedures performed during the first six months is not sufficient to illustrate his or her proficiency, the surgical committee may, upon executive committee approval, extend the period of observation and the proctoring requirement.

The following points must be considered in establishing a proctoring program:

- The system of proctoring may be applied either to all cases performed during the initial six months or to any appropriately selected subsample. For example, the first 10 major abdominal procedures may constitute an appropriate subsample, or five of each of the following orthopedic procedures: laminectomy, total hip replacement, total knee replacement, forearm fracture, intertrochanteric hip repair. One issue that must be resolved by each medical staff and surgical committee is whether it is necessary to require a personal proctor for each minor procedure performed by a new surgeon.

- If proctoring is to be fairly applied, no one surgeon on the staff should be allowed to constantly serve as proctor. New physicians should be instructed to list their preference for proctors evenly among all physicians with similar privileges.

- Proctoring of a specialist previously absent from a community could be performed by any general surgeon. Indepth knowledge of the particular specialty may not be required of the proctor.

- If a newly appointed surgeon's case load extends to two hospitals within the community, the two hospitals may wish to review the aggregate of the new surgeon's cases in order to conduct a more precise review of the total quality of care provided by that physician.

Retrospective review

In the absence of a requirement for personal observation during the initial six months of a new applicant's membership, hospitals may choose to institute a requirement for a retrospective review, or medical care evaluation, of the quality of care provided by that physician. In this situation, all records representing patients treated by the physician would be retrieved from the medical record file and carefully compared with a structured set of audit criteria. The Patient Safety Screening Criteria Set presented in chapter 5, table 5, page 53, may be an appropriate screening mechanism for care provided by newly appointed surgeons.

Once the screening of the charts is completed, those charts that display variance from the criteria should be thoroughly analyzed by the chairman of the department of which the physician is a new member. This analysis of variations from the criteria should also involve several other physicians. The results of this analysis would then be presented to a general staff or medical staff committee meeting.

It is important to emphasize that the use of predetermined criteria to selectively screen medical records does not in any way reduce the need for individual staff physician review of those flagged records. The use of screening criteria simply assists a medical staff committee in gathering uniform data pertaining to a physician's practice. Also, the screening criteria assist in eliminating from review those records that, in all probability, document appropriate medical care.

In the absence of these two systems, a medical staff should at the very least begin to review the quality of a new appointee's practice by subjecting all medical records of patients treated by that physician to physician peer analysis. This peer analysis may be performed by the medical staff as a whole or, if appropriate, it may be performed by a committee of the medical staff. In addition to reviewing the quality of care provided to patients by the physician, the quality, consistency, completeness, and objectivity of the documentation in the medical record by the physician should also be reviewed.

Every hospital with an active medical or surgical audit program can easily begin to review an individual practitioner's performance through the use of predetermined criteria. Charts of a physician in a particular specialty may be easily compared with pre-existing institution-specific criteria relative to that specialty that reflect the generally accepted standard of care for any particular procedure.

In addition to the precise objective evaluation of the quality of care provided by new medical staff applicants, the medical staff should also carefully evaluate a new physician's adherence to basic medical staff rules and regulations. This type of evaluation should be particularly focused upon those rules and regulations that relate to the completion of medical records and those that govern consultations within the institution.

The use of these types of systems—proctoring and retrospective review of new physicians—should greatly reduce the amount of subjectivity involved in the review process. These systems will generate data that demonstrate to the medical staff as a whole that the qualifications, skill, and judgment of each new medical staff member are at, or above, an accepted level of quality. Thus, the medical staff will be taking an active role in preventing medically related patient injuries before they occur.

Emergency Department Credentials Procedure

A logical and practical extension of the observation of new medical staff appointees is the adoption of specific systems to review and ensure the qualifications and skills of new emergency department (ED) physicians prior to the granting of emergency department privileges. As evidence presented in previous chapters demonstrates, this activity is of critical importance, because the ED of a hospital is a unique environment that presents many opportunities for the occurrence of medically related patient injury and malpractice claims.

Several variables combine to make the ED a high-risk area:

- The period of physician-patient contact in the ED is typically brief, and the treatment and attention given the patient are often interrupted several times before completion.
- The vast variety of medical problems seen in the ED can place even the most experienced physician or nurse in an unfamiliar clinical situation.
- ED physicians generally are an extremely mobile group. Consequently, hospital EDs often experience high rates of physician turnover in short periods, which makes it particularly difficult for hospitals to review and verify the qualifications and skills of each new physician applying for ED privileges.

Despite this latter complication, it is absolutely necessary that the medical staff and the chairman of the ED review and ensure the qualifications and practical emergency department skills of every new applicant for emergency department privileges prior to granting ED privileges.

In order to accomplish this, procedures must be instituted to obtain and confirm pertinent information about each ED applicant. Figure 9, page 84, presents an ED information sheet, to be completed by every physician applying for ED privileges. In addition to this information, each hospital should require new applicants to complete an ED physicians' skills list, presented in figure 10, page 85.

Once these forms have been completed, the information contained in them must be verified to the maximum degree possible. Then the executive committee of the medical staff and the chairman of the ED can make an informed decision as to which, if any, ED privileges should be granted to the new applicant. Categories of ED privileges, such as those presented in figure 11, page 88, may be used by hospitals to make the level of ED privileges granted commensurate with the qualifications, ED experience, and skill of the applicant.

Medical Staff Rules and Regulations

Through medical staff rules and regulations, each hospital can significantly reduce the potential for patient injury and the exposure to malpractice liability for specific procedures or activities. The following are examples of such procedures or activities that medical staffs should consider incorporating into their rules and regulations. The need for policies in these and other areas is obvious, yet many hospitals consistently take the path of least resistance and deal with these issues on an individual case basis or not at all.

- *Sponge and instrument counts.* Many hospitals currently have a policy and procedure regarding sponge and instrument counts during surgery. Unfortunately, many hospitals have not taken the next logical and more important step—that of requiring an X ray to be ordered in the event a sponge or instrument count does not coincide with the preoperative count. Enforcement of this policy can be left up to the hospital operating room staff, with the backing of the chairman of the department of surgery.

- *Use of selected antibiotics.* The aminoglycosides comprise a powerful and useful drug group. Their use must, however, be carefully controlled by hospital medical staff in order to reserve these potent drugs for the treatment of infections resistant to other types of antibiotic therapy. Many hospitals are beginning to completely restrict the use of amikacin in order that this drug might be held in reserve for use in combating infections resistant to all other antibiotics. In some instances, the use of gentamicin and tobramycin should be controlled in relation to one another to permit the use of one antibiotic in the hospital and to discourage the use of the other. An individual physician choosing to order the restricted antibiotic may do so but should realize in advance that a policy exists that requires patients' charts relevant to those orders to be carefully reviewed by the pharmacy and therapeutics committee.

- *Writing of inpatient orders by emergency department physicians.* The degree to which ED physicians may write orders affecting patients admitted through the ED should be carefully governed by a policy and procedure developed by the medical staff. Such orders should not be permitted to stand beyond a reasonable period after admission, particularly in special care units. The adherence to these orders may place the patient in serious jeopardy should a complication arise that may be exacerbated by an existing order.

- *The responsibility of the emergency department to assess and render treatment to all ED patients.* The practice of permitting ED physician staff to see certain patients while restricting, via medical staff policy, their ability to assess and administer care to other patients on the basis of their ability to pay must be discouraged. The responsibility of the hospital in this situation is clear. A growing body of case law holds that prompt medical attention must be rendered to ED patients regardless of their admitting physician or payment source. A hospital emergency department should be completely free of restraint in its ability to assess and render lifesaving aid to its patients.

- *A strict policy in regard to the reviewing of all medical staff files.* Information contained in the medical staff files and in minutes of medical staff meetings may be of such a nature that its inappropriate review could lead to substantial litigation problems for the hospital and/or medical staff. Figure 12, page 89, provides a sample policy governing the release of medical staff information and the review of medical staff minutes.

Checklist For High-Risk Surgical Procedures

In terms of both injury frequency and severity, certain surgical procedures carry significantly greater risks of patient injury than do others. These surgical procedures are therefore more likely than are others to generate malpractice liability. In the past, these high-risk surgical procedures were occasionally the topics of retrospective criterion-based reviews conducted by the hospital's quality assurance program. Although these retrospective reviews affirmed an awareness of the risks associated with these surgical procedures, they rarely resulted in the reduction of either the risks associated with, or the frequency of performance of, any given high-risk surgical procedure.

To more directly address the possibility of these risks and reduce them, medical staffs should strongly consider adopting a policy that advocates the voluntary use of checklists, or procedure-indications guidelines, prior to conducting certain surgical procedures. This policy would encourage an attending surgeon to complete a procedure-specific checklist at least 24 hours prior to a scheduled surgery and then to forward the checklist to the chief of surgery.

In a certain few instances, a surgery might be cancelled based upon information elicited by the checklist, but this is not the main purpose of the checklist. Rather, the real purpose of the checklist is to reinforce for each surgeon what the indications for various high-risk surgeries are and to guide each surgeon through an introspective review of the necessity and appropriateness of each high-risk surgical procedure *prior* to its performance. Also, the checklist serves the purpose of developing supportive documentation to validate the indications for the procedure. Figure 13, page 90, is an example of a checklist regarding the indications for the surgical procedure of lumbar laminectomy.

Medical staffs should use several sources to determine which surgical procedures warrant the construction and use of such checklists. These sources include the hospitals' malpractice claims experience in relation to surgical procedures, the hospitals' data (generated by the incident reporting system) regarding frequency and severity of surgical procedure-associated patient injuries, and external data sources that identify high-risk surgical procedures based on nationwide malpractice claims and patient injury data.

The items on each checklist may be developed by adapting justification criteria from retrospective criteria sets, or by a conference of the surgeons who perform each procedure, or by a combination of the two.

Once checklists are implemented for high-risk surgical procedures, the medical staff may wish to extend its use to other high-risk, nonsurgical procedures or activities, for example, the use of selected antibiotics such as the aminoglycosides or the cephalosporins.

INCIDENT REPORTING

Traditional methods of incident reporting and their many flaws were reviewed at length in chapter 4. Past flaws notwithstanding, incident reporting is absolutely critical to the functioning of a viable risk management/patient-injury prevention program.

One major purpose of such a program is to identify and eliminate the occurrence of incidents involving patient injury. To meet this goal, it is imperative that internal mechanisms exist *and are employed* to reliably identify actual problems in patient care or potential risk circumstances. These mechanisms must also accurately and reliably identify instances of patient injury that have already occurred.

Effective medically related incident reporting fulfills two immediately critical functions. It enables the medical staff to actively investigate and identify the cause of incidents and initiate corrective action to eliminate or reduce their future occurrence. It will also enable the risk manager to thoroughly investigate serious incidents to prepare an appropriate defense strategy *prior* to the receipt of a malpractice liability claim.

Effective medically related incident reporting also enables the hospital to achieve the following:

- The building of trend data in relation to number, type, location, and disposition of incidents
- The establishment of hospitalwide standards of care
- The minimization of malpractice claims
- The continual reduction of the frequency and severity of patient injuries

Each hospital must first draft, adopt, and distribute its own definition of an incident or adverse patient occurrence. Next, and more important, each hospital must establish and distribute guidelines that state what specific circumstances or occurrences warrant the completion of an incident report. For specific occurrences or patient injuries, guidelines should be distributed that require the completion of an incident report.

For example, an incident might be defined as any occurrence, accident, or event, including a medically related occurrence, that is not consistent with the provision of normal patient care, that did or could result in an injury to a patient.

Once an incident is defined and everyone in the institution is informed of the definition, guidelines must be developed and distributed that help determine under what circumstances an incident report should be completed.

Regardless of what type of incident report form is used or whether incidents may be verbally reported, hospitalwide guidelines such as the following must be used to ensure the generation of medically related incident reports.

Medication Errors

Incident reports must be made for all occurrences of omitted doses, misread orders, errors in medication administration, incorrect dosage administration, medication administered to the wrong patient, transciption errors, verbal medication orders, medication not administered at the date and time prescribed (plus or minus one hour), allergic or adverse drug reactions, mechanical failures, charting errors, pharmacy errors, and patient errors. The American College of Surgeons (1979) points out that medication errors envelop a wider possible range of abnormal occurrences than does any other category of incident. For this reason, it may be useful for hospitals to construct a medication error report form that is separate and distinct from the general incident report form.

The separate medication error form will permit hospitals to collect and analyze continuing medication error data independently of other incident report data. This will expedite the identification of problem trends associated with medication administration and will suggest courses of corrective action to reverse those trends and prevent patient injuries before they occur. In addition, the actual use of separate report forms for medication errors will emphasize the seriousness of this problem to the nursing and medical staff, and may in itself help reverse negative trends (American College of Surgeons, 1979).

Incidents Related to Intravenous Medication

If intravenous medication (IV) incidents are considered as separate from

medication error incidents, then incident reports must be made for all occurrences of IV infusion rate not within 10 percent of that specified over
a 24-hour period; infiltration characterized by edema of 3 centimeters or
greater and accompanied by tenderness and pain; edema of less that 3 cm
when a drug diluted in less that 250 millimeters of solution has been in-
filtrated; infiltration of a known tissue-damaging drug regardless of the
dilution of the drug; phlebitis of 2 cm or greater extending along the
catherized vein beyond the puncture; or any unusual event (such as
runaway IVs).

Hospital-Incurred Traumas

Incident reports must be made for all occurrences of any fall or collision;
any burn, whether electrical, chemical, or other; any trauma involving
lacerations that require sutures; any other event considered traumatic in
nature. Such events have comprised the main volume of traditional incident reporting. Although slips and falls are not of primary concern in a
medically directed patient injury prevention program, they obviously
relate to patient injury and should be investigated. It should be made
clear to all staff, however, that this is only one of many categories of occurrences that warrants incident reporting, and that to identify slips and
falls is not the major purpose of incident reporting.

Potentially Compensable Events or Unusual Occurrences

Incident reports must be made for all occurrences of unplanned second
operative procedures performed during a single admission; unscheduled
removal of an organ during surgery; unscheduled repair of an organ during surgery; patient death; patients discharged from hospital with infections or on intramuscular medications; unusual documentation in or
evidence of tampering with a medical record; any patient discussing
potential lawsuits against physicians, nurses, or the hospital; any complaint of improper treatment made by the patient or the patient's family
or attorney. This and all other categories of guidelines must be expanded
individually by each hospital. A good source for inclusions in this
category are the criteria from the "Patient Safety Screening Criteria" set
presented in chapter 5, table 5, page 53.

Department-Specific Guidelines

In addition, through active departmental involvement, each hospital
should also construct department-specific or procedure-specific guidelines that assist in identifying those incidents or occurrences that must be
reported. Adopting this type of specific guideline system will reduce the
potential for conflict between professionals that may be generated by

uncertainty as to whether an incident or occurrence report should be completed or not. It will also ensure that the majority of serious medically related occurrences are indeed reported. It is imperative that all members of any particular department agree upon or participate in the modification of the set of department-specific incident report guidelines. It is equally important that all members of a given department realize that incident reports must be routinely completed when a situation described in the guidelines occurs.

On the basis of a hospital's own claims and patient-injury history, it should decide which departments warrant the immediate construction of incident reporting guidelines. For example, these departments might initially include: labor and delivery, anesthesiology, the emergency department, and the surgical suite.

The department-specific incident reporting guidelines will indicate what occurrences in particular departments must be documented in an incident report. It must be completely understood by each member of the department that the completion of an incident report does not indicate fault but is part of the hospital's risk management system, which is, in part, designed to protect the hospital, the medical staff, and the employees in the event a malpractice claim is filed. It must be further understood that the incident report is not generally used punitively but is used to identify areas of potentially high liability and to initiate methods to eliminate or minimize the potential risk.

Figure 14, page 91, and figure 15, page 92, are two examples of incident reporting guidelines for two departments that generally have a high potential for causing patient injuries and for generating malpractice liability claims: the emergency department and the surgical suite.

These guidelines are presented as examples only. Whereas hospitals may incorporate them into their own incident reporting guidelines, each department must expand and revise the guidelines to be department-specific and to reflect individual institutional practice patterns. This will ensure that the guidelines are meaningful and valid and that each member of the department is aware of and has given approval to the guidelines and the purpose of incident reporting. It also will result in the generation of incident reports that yield data instrumental to the prevention of medically related patient injuries.

In addition to the type of guidelines presented in figures 14, page 91, and 15, page 92, hospitals may wish to place maximum limits on certain dynamic departmental variables to act as nonspecific, but nevertheless valuable, guidelines for the completion of incident reports. For example, the department of anesthesiology could establish a maximum anesthesia administration time for types of operative procedures, so that the event of any patient anesthetized longer than this set time would initiate the completion of an incident report. The department of surgery might establish a maximum estimated intraoperative blood loss per procedure so that any blood loss over the specified amount would require the completion of an incident report.

Occurrences or events that are not listed in the guidelines may still justify incident reporting. All medical and nursing staff and all relevant employees should be encouraged to report any occurrence not listed in the guidelines if they believe reporting is warranted. It must be clearly understood, however, that any occurrence listed in the guidelines mandates that an incident report must be completed.

Processing Incident Reports

As a general rule, all incident reports should be completed and routed to the appropriate individual within 24 hours of the occurrence or the discovery of the incident. Once incident guidelines are established, hospitals may wish to consider permitting incidents to be reported in verbal, rather than written, form.

The medical staff of the hospital must approve the routing procedure of incident report information. For example, it may be decided that all incident reports will first go to the risk manager for triage. The risk manager might then involve appropriate department heads and a specified member of the hospital administration to determine what, if any, courses of corrective action may be necessary. If there is a suspicion that distilled incident report information represents significant problem trends in patient care, it may be shared with the quality assurance department. On the basis of this information, the quality assurance department may initiate an indepth evaluation of the problem and pass the results of the evaluation back to the risk manager.

Regardless of the routing procedure agreed upon, it is critically important that the information contained on incident reports not be freely distributed or easily accessible. The more accessible incident report information is, the less likely physicians and nurses will be to identify medically related patient injuries. To ensure the generation and validity of incident reports, each hospital must institute rigid routing procedures for incident report information and must restrict the number of copies of incident reports to a minimum.

To conclude, a hospital's incident reporting system will function effectively only if everyone engaged in the provision of patient care understands and complies with the following:

- The purposes of incident reporting
- The hospital's definition of an incident

- That guidelines exist to specify under what circumstances an incident report must be completed
- Who is responsible for making an incident report
- That the completed incident reports follow a tightly controlled routing path, are kept confidential, and are inaccessible to all but authorized persons
- The types of corrective action that can be generated by incident reports, and the understanding that this corrective action is generally nonpunitive
- That incident reporting plays a significant role in the prevention of medically related patient injuries, and that it can therefore help improve the quality of care and reduce the risk of malpractice claims

SPECIAL STUDIES AND USE OF OUTSIDE CONSULTANTS

As medical technology becomes more advanced and as the practice of medicine within hospitals becomes more complicated and specialized, medical staffs will experience a growing need for outside assistance in the review of certain situations or departments. This type of review will provide the medical staff with needed feedback from special areas regarding the quality of care rendered and the potential for patient injury and malpractice liability. Examples of situations that might require the use of special studies or outside consultants include:

- A 150-bed community hospital with one orthopedist on staff. Who reviews the quality of care provided by this practitioner? What evidence is there that new orthopedic techniques and practices are being learned and employed by this practitioner? What is the medical staff's malpractice liability exposure and responsibility in this situation?
- A 350-bed community hospital in which only one physician has privileges to perform gastroscopies, fiberoptic bronchoscopies, or other procedures. How does the medical staff ensure that the quality of care provided by this physician is optimal? Who reviews the continuing performance of a practitioner who has traditionally been the only physician in a particular setting responsible for those activities?
- A 250-bed hospital with three radiologists on staff, who make up a relatively long-term group at the hospital. What provision exists for review of the quality of the procedure or the interpretation of the X ray? How does the medical staff appraise the degree of skill of the radiology group? What internal provisions exist to point out inconsistencies with interpretations or problems existing within that group?

- A 315-bed community hospital with four independently practicing obstetric/gynecological specialists on the staff. Two of these practitioners are constantly suggesting that a third is providing poor or substandard care. The fourth practitioner refuses to make any comment on, or review of, the quality of care provided by the third. The medical staff must resolve the issue. Who will provide a non-biased review of the practice of the obstetrical specialty to the executive committee?
- A 415-bed hospital that has a contract with a single practitioner to interpret electroencephalograms (EEGs). What assurance does the medical staff have that the individual who reviews EEGs is not consistently misinterpreting or underreading them? Is the medical staff as a whole able to evaluate the quality of care provided by this practitioner or should an alternative mechanism be used?
- A 200-bed rural hospital that has a contract with an emergency physicians group to provide 24-hour service to the emergency department. The medical staff consistently questions the quality of care provided by the ED physicians, yet lacks any objective documentation to substantiate this claim. The administration and the medical staff jointly agree that there needs to be some evaluation in this particular area and are unable to agree on the approach to be taken.

Each of these situations might best be approached through the use of a physician consultant from another community or perhaps from the nearest university hospital. Hospitals currently rely upon a wide range of outside consultants to assist them in reviewing various types of services. These services include hospital laboratory reviews, financial management reviews, and hospital management services. Generally, surveys and services traditionally performed by outside consultants do not review the quality of patient care provided by practitioners in the hospital. This type of evaluation is the responsibility of the hospital board and is generally delegated to the medical staff. It is therefore usually performed internally. As the preceding examples suggest, however, certain situations indicate the need for clinically oriented surveys, performed by external consultants, to assist the medical executive committee and the administration in the identification and resolution of clinical problems.

Such external consultations, as well as specialty criteria sets for retrospective reviews, are usually available through large university hospitals or through private medical consulting firms. These services are expensive and should be chosen carefully to fulfill a demonstrated need. In order to maintain objectivity, each external surveyor should have no more than a minimal knowledge of the practitioners in the particular hospital and should be provided with a statistically valid sample of patient records for review. The medical executive committee must specifically authorize each external consultant to assist it in clinical reviews and must ensure that the results of the reviews are maintained as part of the hospital's quality assurance documentation to provide confidentiality. Most states have passed provisions that extend immunity to outside consultants assisting a medical staff in the review of the quality of care. These provisions protect the consultants from most legal actions resulting from the initiation of corrective action, such as the suspension of a physician's privileges.

Several examples follow of the types of external consultations hospitals currently use. In each instance, the hospital had a need for requesting the external consultations and processed the survey results within the organized structure of the medical staff. Documentation of these surveys was maintained as medical staff, not administrative, documentation and was reported in summary form to the board of directors of each hospital.

- A radiology group in a 310-bed hospital periodically arranges for twice monthly visits by two university-associated radiologists. One of the radiologists, a specialist in computed tomography (CT) interpretation, provides onsite reinterpretation of all CT examinations performed during the preceding period and participates with the radiology group in in-service education on CT interpretation. The second radiologist, also affiliated with a medical school, provides direct input into the type of radiological procedures used at the hospital and regularly rereads a selected sample of films taken during the prior period. In each instance, any inconsistencies that are identified with the radiological interpretations are immediately analyzed by the group and pointed out to the attending physician responsible for the patient. These activities are documented, by means of a simple system, and may help satisfy the documentation required by the Joint Commission on Accreditation of Hospitals for quality assurance and in-service and continuing medical education.

- Another hospital regularly submits 50 to 200 EEG strips to an outside specialist for reinterpretation. Once the hospital receives these reinterpretations, the medical executive committee carefully compares them with the initial interpretations provided by the staff of physician specialists. The resultant report assures the hospital that the interpretations of EEGs provided to attending physicians are accurate and assist physicians in establishing appropriate diagnoses and therapy. In at least one instance during the past three years, the results of these external evaluations have prompted the medical executive committee to request further continuing medical education and a more precise documentation of a specific problem identified on the strip.

In addition, medical staffs are beginning to request complete external evaluations of the quality of care and documentation provided by emergency department physicians. Such external studies directly assist the medical executive committee in identifying areas of major patient injury potential within the emergency department, and also assist in the prompt correction of recognized deficiencies. The use of outside consultants in this particular area is encouraged, as the possibility for subjective, counterproductive review exists if a medical staff attempts to review its own emergency department. On the other hand, asking an emergency department to demonstrate evidence of its own quality subjects the review to charges of subjectivity and may not in any way help to prevent the occurrence of patient injuries.

Studies such as these, although not yet common in this country, are beginning to play a greater role in hospital quality assurance and patient injury prevention activities. Of paramount importance in the use of external consultants is the responsibility of the organized medical staff for the initial design of the study and for the receipt and evaluation of the results. Corrective action based upon the study results can range from simple information dissemination to the elimination of staff privileges for a practitioner.

Reference

American College of Surgeons, in consultation with the Maryland Hospital Education Institute. *Patient Safety Manual: A Guide for Establishing a Patient Safety System in Your Hospital.* Chicago: ACS, 1979.

Dear _____ :

Dr. _____ has recently applied to join the medical
staff of Memorial Hospital and has indicated to us that he was
previously a member of your hospital staff.

In order to effectively evaluate Dr. _____'s clinical
abilities and credentials, we would very much appreciate receiving
your candid evaluation of him. Additionally, could you please
complete the attached information form pertaining to Dr._____.

We wish to thank you in advance for assisting us in this matter
and realize that this request may take up valuable time. However,
be assured that you will receive equal value in the event that you
or your staff request a similar reference from us in the future.

                                        Sincerely Yours

                                        MEMORIAL HOSPITAL

                                        _____
                                        Administrator

Enclosures

Figure 4
Form Letter Requesting References

Dr._____   Date of application: _____
    (applicant)

To be completed by reference:

1. Applicant was on the staff of _____Hospital between _____ and _____.

2. Applicant had privileges in the following field(s): _____, _____, _____, _____.

3. Applicant was on the staff of the following institutions as well as ours: __
   _____

4. Did applicant ever have his privileges to admit or treat patients suspended, revoked, or withdrawn at any time while on your staff? (Please ignore temporary suspensions due to failure to complete medical records)

   ☐ Yes   ☐ No

   If yes, please explain _____
   _____
   _____.

5. To your knowledge has applicant been involved in any successful malpractice claim or action while a member of your medical staff?

   ☐ Yes   ☐ No

   If yes, please explain _____
   _____
   _____
   _____
   _____

Thank you very much for your answers to these questions. Please use the reverse side of the questionnaire to give us your candid evaluation of this applicant's clinical abilities while a member of your staff in addition to any other comments you feel may help us make an appropriate evaluation of his clinical abilities and/or other skills.

_____
Signature

_____
Title

Figure 5
Medical Staff Questionnaire

Physician _____ Date of application _____

Applying for privileges in _____, _____

AMA request sent _____returned _____

Malpractice insurance carrier_____City_____State_____

Letters of recommendation sent to:

Date	Reference	Returned
_____	_____	_____
_____	_____	_____
_____	_____	_____
_____	_____	_____
_____	_____	_____

Application review and personal interview with credentials
committee: _____
               Date

Privileges delineated by Dr. _____chairman/dept. of _____

Privileges:	Temporary _____	MEC approval _____	Board _____
	Associate _____	" " _____	" _____
	Active _____	" " _____	" _____
	Courtesy _____	" " _____	" _____

REAPPOINTMENT

Reappointment application sent: _____Returned _____

Complete: Yes ☐   No ☐

Sent to Director of Medical Affairs   _____
Sent to Department Chairman   _____
Sent to Credentials Committee   _____
Sent to Executive Committee   _____
Sent to Board   _____

Reappointment granted: Yes ☐   No ☐

Privileges granted: _____

Figure 6
Form for Monitoring Initial Appointment to the Medical Staff

Dear Doctor _____ :

The Surgical Committee wishes to welcome you to our hospital. As you know, our medical staff bylaws require a period of observation prior to approval for full nonproctored surgical privileges. During a minimum of the first six months of your practice here at the hospital it will be necessary for you to obtain a proctor to supervise your surgical care and operative proficiency on each case you perform. You should keep a list of these cases as well as the physician who proctored you at that time. The purpose of this procedure is to satisfy the committee's obligation to assure the medical community that you are proficient in your specialty. You should make every effort to diversify your preceptors so that no one physician has observed the majority of your cases.

When you feel your experience has been broad enough to warrant consideration for full surgical privileges, you may then apply to the committee. Your application should include a list of cases, including the name of the proctor for each individual case. The operating room staff is instructed to require that a proctor is present during any operative procedure you perform. It is not the obligation of the operating room staff to find a proctor for you, and you should do this ahead of time, giving adequate notice to the surgeon involved.

If I can be of any assistance to you in your start here at _____ Hospital, please feel free to call on me.

                              Sincerely,

                              Chairman,
                              Surgical Department

cc: Chief Executive Officer
     Director of Medical Affairs

Figure 7
Sample Surgical Proctor Letter

Patient # _____   Your name _____   ED Case
Surgeon _____   Date and time _____
Procedure _____   Yes ____No ____

Preoperative

1) History and physical on chart and complete   Yes ☐ No ☐ _____
2) Progress note(s) regarding planned procedure   Yes ☐ No ☐ _____
3) Preoperative justification for surgery
   documented (both objective and/or subjective) Yes ☐ No ☐ _____
4) Proper consent and explanation of risks
   documented   Yes ☐ No ☐ _____

General comment: _____
_____

Intraoperative

Please comment on the following if applicable (timeliness of surgery,
anesthesia, technical skill, knowledge of procedure, responsiveness to
operating room staff, blood loss, surgical judgment, and so forth)

Comment: _____
_____

Postoperative

1) Preoperative diagnosis coincides with
   postoperative findings   Yes ☐   No ☐ ____
2) Postoperative care adequate   Yes ☐   No ☐ ____
3) Operative report complete, accurate, and
   timely   Yes ☐   No ☐ ____
4) Disposition of patient appropriate   Yes ☐   No ☐ ____
5) Complications (if any) recognized and
   managed appropriately   Yes ☐   No ☐ ____

General comment on the handling of this case: _____
_____
_____

NOTE: Thank you very much for your assistance in reviewing this physician. Your comments are of great value to the Surgical Committee.

RETURN TO:_____

Figure 8
Sample Surgical Proctor's Report

Name: _____ Date: _____
        (applicant)

To be completed by applicant:

1. Please list in chronological order hospital/practice settings worked in during the past five years (with dates): _____,
_____, _____,
_____, _____.

2. Please list areas in which you currently have hospital privileges:

_____, _____, _____,
_____, _____, _____.

3. Approximate number of hours engaged in emergency department medicine practice in the last year: _____.

4. Have you ever been involved in a successful malpractice action? _____
If "yes," please explain _____.
Have you ever had your privileges to practice medicine/surgery revoked or suspended in any way?_____ If "yes," please explain_____
_____.

5. The last emergency department I worked in had an annual volume of _____ patients of which approximately _____% were admitted to the hospital after emergency treatment.

6. During the past two years I have been a member of the following medical staff committees: _____, _____, _____, _____.

7. During the past year I have attended the following courses pertinent to emergency medicine: _____
_____
_____
_____
_____

Figure 9
Emergency Department Information Sheet

Please check the appropriate column for the skills listed below: .

I have done within last six months and approximate number of times	I was trained to do but haven't yet done	Skills
____ ____	_____	Abcess, incision and drainage
____ ____	_____	Advanced life support
____ ____	_____	Arthrocentesis (emergency only) of:
____ ____	_____	Elbow
____ ____	_____	Knee
____ ____	_____	Immobilization and splinting of fractures
____ ____	_____	Central venous pressure catheter placement
____ ____	_____	Closed emergency reduction of dislocations
____ ____	_____	Digit
____ ____	_____	Elbow
____ ____	_____	Patella
____ ____	_____	Shoulder
____ ____	_____	Cricothyrotomy and tracheostomy
____ ____	_____	Emergency immobilization techniqes and transportation
____ ____	_____	Endotracheal intubation
____ ____	_____	Epistaxis, coagulation for
____ ____	_____	Heimlich maneuver
____ ____	_____	Intracardiac injection
____ ____	_____	Intravenous puncture by one of the four following routes:
____ ____	_____	Cutdown
____ ____	_____	External jugular
____ ____	_____	Scalp
____ ____	_____	Subclavian

Figure 10
Skills List for Emergency Department Physicians

I have done within last six months and approximate number of times	I was trained to do but haven't yet done	Skills
____ ____	_____	Foreign body removal
____ ____	_____	Lacerations, repair of
____ ____	_____	Laryngoscopy:
____ ____	_____	Direct (in emergency only)
____ ____	_____	Indirect
____ ____	_____	Lumbar puncture
____ ____	_____	Nail trephination and nail bed removal
____ ____	_____	Nasal packs:
____ ____	_____	Anterior
____ ____	_____	Posterior
____ ____	_____	Paracentesis
____ ____	_____	Pericardiocentesis
____ ____	_____	Peritoneal lavage (after speaking with attending physician)
____ ____	_____	Preservation of severed extremities:
____ ____	_____	(ear, nose, penis)
____ ____	_____	Regional block anesthesia:
____ ____	_____	Digital and intercostal
____ ____	_____	Field
____ ____	_____	Anoscopy for rectal bleeding
____ ____	_____	Slit lamps
____ ____	_____	Split thickness grafting
____ ____	_____	Surgical debridement
____ ____	_____	Thoracentesis
____ ____	_____	Thoracotomy tube, insertion of
____ ____	_____	Tonometry, ocular
____ ____	_____	Urethral catheter, use of
____ ____	_____	Blocks:
____ ____	_____	Facial (supraorbital, infraorbital alvelar, and submental)

Figure 10
Skills List for Emergency Department Physicians (cont.)

I have done within last six months and approximate number of times	I was trained to do but haven't yet done	Skills
____ ____	_____	Blocks:
____ ____	_____	Radial, ulnar, median
____ ____	_____	Military antishock trousers—gravity suit, application
____ ____	_____	Transtracheal aspiration
____ ____	_____	Urethral sounds and filiforms

Physician's signature
_____

Date

Figure 10
Skills List for Emergency Department Physicians (cont.)

1. Unrestricted privileges in emergency medicine

2. Privileges in emergency medicine with either concurrent or retrospective monitoring or both: probationary

3. Privileges in emergency medicine restricted to practice only when on duty with a category I ED physician

NOTES: 1. No ED physician may treat patients on an inpatient basis (exception, cardiac arrests).

2. Appropriate assistance must be requested in all major trauma, coronary, and psychiatric cases.

3. Any ED physician can exercise the prerogative to render lifesaving care any time it is needed. The delineation of these privileges is in no way intended to interfere with lifesaving measures.

Figure 11
Emergency Department Privilege Categories

Purpose:

This policy on release of medical staff committee minutes has been adopted to preserve the confidentiality of all medical staff activities and to prevent unauthorized distribution of medical staff committee minutes in the hope of reducing to a minimum the likelihood that these minutes will inadvertently be left in locations frequented by individuals not authorized to read them.

Functional:

Medical Staff Committee minutes will not be released in written form unless requested by:

- President of the Staff
- Director of Medical Affairs
- Chairman of the committee responsible for the generation of said minutes
- President or Vice-President(s) of the hospital.

Originals and all copies wil be filed in the Medical Staff Office only. All copies will be made by and returned to the Medical Staff Office unless they are to be incorporated in other committee minutes. A record of all releases will be maintained.

Any physician member of _____ Hospital's medical staff may review any set of minutes at any time, provided they are not removed from the file.

Responsibility:

Director of Medical Affairs and Vice-President for Professional Services

Figure 12
Sample Policy on the Release of Medical Staff
Committee Information

A. One or more of the following:

  1. Myelogram positive for total block, indentation of filling defect corresponding to clinical suspicion of level of intervertebral disc involvement ☐ Yes

  2. Positive electromyogram more than three weeks after onset of denervation corresponding to clinical suspicion of level of intervertebral disc involvement ☐ Yes

  3. Discography report positive for pathologic disc ☐ Yes

AND

B. One or more of the following:

  1. Decreasing to absent bladder/bowel function ☐ Yes

  2. Unremitting back or leg pain ☐ Yes

  3. Decreased deep tendon reflexes (DTR) (depressed, hypoactive, or absent knee or ankle jerks) ☐ Yes

  4. Measurable muscle atrophy ☐ Yes

AND

C. At least 10 days of total bed rest documented in record ☐ Yes

---

If laminectomy is being performed for a reason other than the above, please explain: (here or in record)

_____

_____

_____

_____

_____

Figure 13
Checklist for Lumbar Laminectomy Surgery

1. Patient discharged without being seen by physician
   A. *Except* if phone order of private physician or order originating at a private physician's office is acceptable; no incident report necessary.
   B. *Except* if patient decides treatment/examination not necessary after being admitted to ED. *Patient's choice* must be noted on chart; no incident report necessary.
2. Return to ED for same injury/illness—condition worsened
   A. *Except* when advised to return by physician on initial visit, for example, abdominal pain; rule out appendicitis, wound infection, wound check; no incident report necessary
   B. *Except* if return to ED is due to incidental disease discovery, for example, lung tumor found on X ray of injured ribs, and so forth; no incident report necessary
   C. *Except* if patient was advised to return at a more convenient time for further study/consultation/treatment; no incident report necessary
   D. *Except* when illness prompting initial visit to ED is expected to worsen, for example, burn treatment; no incident report necessary
3. Procedure performed on wrong patient or wrong procedure.
   For example, X ray done on pregnant patient, sutures removed on wound check, wrong medication given to patient
   All require incident report completion
4. No written consent for procedure when consent is necessary
   A. *Except* if emergency consent not deemed necessary by two examining physicians and noted in chart; no incident report necessary
5. Patient refuses to be treated and refuses to sign against medical advice release or chart
6. Allergic or adverse drug reaction to medication given while in ED
7. Death in ED
8. No interpretation of X ray by radiologist within 24 hours of X ray being made
9. Patient visits ED for treatment of complication or adverse result of recent hospitalization (within three months of discharge)

Figure 14
Selected Emergency Department Guidelines for Completion of an
Incident Report

1. Return to operating room for repair or removal of an organ or body part damaged in surgery

2. Unplanned removal or repair of an organ or part of an organ during an operative procedure

3. Acute myocardial infarction *and* a surgical procedure on same admission

4. Neurological deficit not present upon admission or prior to surgery

5. Intraoperative rise in blood pressure requiring intervention such as nitroprusside or diazoxide drip

7. Unplanned return to operating room

8. Patient transferred from operating room to surgical or other intensive care unit
   A. *Except* if patient was admitted to operating from surgical or other intensive care unit; no incident report necessary
   B. *Except* if admission was planned prior to surgery, must be in chart; no incident report necessary

9. Death in operating room

10. Incorrect sponge count and no X ray ordered

11. Incorrect instrument count and no X ray ordered

12. Equipment failure or malfunction during surgery

Figure 15
Selected Operating Room Guidelines for Completion of an
Incident Report

CHAPTER 7

Relating Patient Injury Prevention to Quality Assurance

The conduct of patient injury prevention activities clearly intersects with the quality assurance activities in any given hospital. How these activities should interrelate functionally and organizationally is up to each hospital to decide. Among other things, the decision will be based upon the organizational structure of the hospital, its style of management, and its view of the dynamic relationship between risk management/patient injury prevention and quality assurance. An example follows of how one hospital might approach this organizational relationship. This example is presented for consideration and comparison only; any hospital that wishes to follow this model should carefully revise it to best reflect and respond to its own institutional practice patterns and organizational structure and needs.

QUALITY ASSURANCE OVERVIEW

The purpose of this overview is to describe the mechanisms utilized by a hospital to evaluate, monitor, and improve the quality of patient care at the hospital. This document is not a quality assurance plan; it is a description of the relationship among nonphysician departments, the organized medical staff, and the administration.

In an attempt to unify and coordinate all quality assurance and quality enhancement programs at the hospital, a department of patient care evaluation was created; the department is directed by the vice-president for professional services and the director of medical affairs. Within the department are the following individual positions:

- Coordinator of continuing medical education
- Medical staff secretary
- Quality assurance coordinator/incident report coordinator

- Utilization review coordinator/nurse audit assistant
- Infection control office
- Safety office

The department assists the medical and other professional staffs with all organized quality assurance systems and serves as an integrating force. Periodic meetings held by this department promote coordination and enhance the benefit of all quality assurance activities.

The hospital's quality assurance program is operated through three primary committees: the professional activities of the board; the medical staff executive committee (MEC); the departmental quality assurance committee.

The MEC's functions are described in the medical staff bylaws. These bylaws describe fully six primary components of the quality assurance program: credentialing and privileges delineation, reappraisal and reappointment, continuous monitoring of selected functions (that is, tissue, antibiotics, blood, medical records, and so forth), medical care evaluation, utilization review (admission, length of stay, ancillary services), and continuing medical evaluation.

The bylaws provide for an organized committee structure and lines of communication and specify that the medical staff executive committee assumes an oversight function as well as taking final action on certain recommendations.

The departmental quality assurance committee is the nonphysician counterpart to the MEC and performs a similar function (See Departmental Quality Assurance Plan, following).

Departmental Quality Assurance Plan

This plan outlines the mechanisms used by a hospital to adequately evaluate the quality of patient services. The plan is developed on the basis of the hospital's needs and resources, with the intent of achieving maximum coordination while reducing inefficiencies. The plan describes the mechanisms that are to be utilized to account for care provided and establishes a system to ensure compliance with the plan itself. Lines of communication and authority are described for each component of the hospital (governing body, medical staff, nursing services, allied health professionals, and administration). The systems outlined should lead to effectiveness through information sharing. Additionally, the plan calls for participation by all involved in the delivery of patient care.

Authority

The plan is created under the authority of the hospital's board of directors and the relevant department heads, patient care managers, administration, and medical staff leaders.

Involved departments or functions

The following organizational units participate in implementing the plan: administration, admitting, anesthesia, chaplaincy, development and community relations, dietary, education, EEG, EKG, emergency department, employee health, finance, housekeeping, laboratory, materials management, medical records, medical staff, nuclear medicine, nursing, patient care evaluation, patient education, personnel, pharmacy, public relations, radiology, rehabilitation, respiratory therapy, safety, social services, and volunteers.

Organization and reporting

To provide for effective integration and coordination of hospitalwide quality assurance functions, one departmental meeting per month is used exclusively for quality assurance purposes. During this meeting, progress reports and study summaries are shared when relevant. Quality assurance goals and priorities are to be appraised and constant evaluation and modification of the plan's implementation must be conducted. (For a list of the plan's reporting schedule, see figure 16, below).

Monthly
- Progress reports
- Study summaries
- Continuing education

Bimonthly
- Incident reports
- Infection control
- Patient interviews and complaints

Quarterly
- Allied health professional credentialing
- Reports of external surveys
- Reviews of census and financial data, if not given previously
- Safety committee reports

Figure 16
Schedule of Reports for a Quality Assurance Plan

Each department head makes a verbal summary report of each completed study to the department head group. This summary contains the following information:

- Involved individuals or groups
- The study topic
- The manner in which it was selected (that is, perceived problems, new technique, or follow-up. All studies should be focused upon known or suspected problems; methods used to identify potential problems include review of census data, patient complaints, incident reports, physician reports, other studies, delays in service, and financial data.)
- Objective of study
- Number of records reviewed (or other data reviewed)
- System used to review records (that is, predefined criteria, subjective review, or other)
- Results of review—lack of problems or actual problems discovered
- Suspected cause(s) of problem(s)
- Proposed corrective action
- Follow-up plan or evidence of effectiveness

A written summary is sent to the patient care evaluation department for final submission to the strategic planning committee, medical executive committee, administration, and governing board.

Progress reports

A bimonthly report developed by the patient care evaluation department summarizes the quality assurance activities of all involved departments or individuals. These reports indicate completed studies and studies in progress, as well as inactivity in particular areas. A brief report of problems identified is included along with actions recommended.

Methods of review

All studies performed consist of the following six essential characteristics:

1. Study design (including topic selection, objective setting, and study size)
2. Review parameters (such as predetermined clinical criteria and numerical guidelines)
3. Analysis of records or data
4. Problem identification
5. Corrective action, recommendations, and follow-up plan
6. Summary report

Documentation of each step must be maintained in at least summary form. Individual studies may be performed on as few as 10 records or as many as 100. Large studies (that is, 50 records or more) should be preceded by a study of 10 records to assess the effectiveness of the criteria and study topic.

The method used by individual departments to perform the review of patient care may vary; retrospective, concurrent, or prospective assessment is permitted. No one system of audit or evaluation is required by this plan; however, each department submits its own policy and procedure for patient care evaluation. These policies and procedures outline in general terms the frequency of evaluation efforts (a minimum of four per year or to include at least 15 percent of the patients served) and the interdepartmental handling of each study.

Cooperation and coordination

Departments can cooperate on any number of studies if the topic is pertinent to each. For example, on a cardiovascular accident study, there can be cooperation by physical, occupational, and speech therapy; nursing; and dietary.

In the event of such cooperation, each participating department can report separately. Additionally, each receives credit for its participation. Departments are strongly encouraged to involve members of the medical staff in their evaluation activities. Furthermore, departments may elect to perform studies in cooperation with other hospitals or groups (see "Confidentiality," page 98). This type of sharing is encouraged by this plan.

Quality Assurance Components

Regular objective evaluation

Audit, medical care evaluation studies, performance evaluation procedures, and other similar activities are all formal review systems. These or modifications of them may be used to perform necessary studies, reported quarterly by department heads.

Patient interviews and complaints

Reports on these activities are summarized quarterly by the department responsible for public relations and are presented for information and possible action.

Infection control

Bimonthly reports on hospital infections by unit or department are presented along with major actions taken by the infection control committee.

Incident reporting

Verbal reports of frequently occurring incidents are presented bimonthly, along with pertinent actions taken by the safety committee.

Allied health professional credentialing

The medical staff regularly reviews credentials of selected allied health professionals and assigns privileges. Quarterly reports of this activity are presented to the department head group for comment and input.

Continuing education

Ongoing reports are presented of all education programs that result from patient care evaluation activities.

Review of census and financial data

As necessary, various relevant data are presented by the finance department pertaining to patient care practice.

Reports of external surveys

All surveys performed by external groups are reviewed as received when they are pertinent to the quality of patient care.

Safety committee reports

All minutes and results of internal surveys are reviewed by the department head group.

Problem resolution

Appropriate corrective action is recommended and implemented to eliminate or reduce any problems identified as a result of any quality assurance activity. Such actions can include but need not be limited to the following: educational and training programs, development and implementation of new or revised policies and procedures, staffing changes, equipment or facility changes, counseling or individual guidance, and adjustment in hospital duties or privileges.

Confidentiality

Maximum confidentiality must be maintained if departmental quality assurance activities are to be effective. However, unnecessary restriction on the use of quality assurance results should be avoided. Mutual respect and cognizance of the sensitivity of quality assurance information should generally govern the release of information. In addition, the following provisions must be observed by all individuals engaged in the hospital quality assurance effort:

- Any report submitted to a group other than the department head group will be cleared by the strategic planning committee.

- All studies performed in conjunction with other hospitals will be cleared by the department head group.
- No study will be initiated and performed by one individual (unless a department head) without the consent of the department head group. (All studies should be performed by a department, special committee, or standing committee.)

Administrative involvement

The administration must encourage and support all activities designed to enhance the quality of patient care services provided at the hospital. Appropriate support staff should be allocated for these functions as needed by the department head group. Administration should foster appropriate activities by emphasizing individual responsibility for the quality of patient care services provided within a particular area and group responsibility for the overall effectiveness of the quality assurance program. The encouragement and support of administration must not be interpreted as indicative of assumption of any quality assurance activities by the administration.

Evaluation of the quality assurance program

The department head group, the administration, the medical staff, and the governing board review the effectiveness of the quality assurance plan at three-month intervals to ensure that the collective effort is comprehensive, shows minimal duplication of effort, is cost effective, and results in demonstrable improvements in patient care. This reappraisal attempts to identify components of the quality assurance program that need to be designed and instituted, altered, or deleted. During this yearly evaluation, emphasis is placed on overall effectiveness of the program, as demonstrated through problem identification and resolution. From the onset, it is understood and agreed that not all quality assurance studies will disclose problems. Many studies will simply identify that the quality of patient care is high and thus serve as appropriate assurance for the governing board.

Plan approval

The plan is carefully reviewed by each of the participating departments or individuals and is specifically approved by each department head, the administration, the medical staff leadership, and the governing board. Amendments to this plan may be made from time to time if, in the opinion of the department head group, such amendments are likely to be conducive to improved evaluation of patient care.

DEVELOPING EDUCATION PROGRAMS
FOR PREVENTING PATIENT INJURY

Internal information dissemination and education regarding the purposes, systems, and techniques of patient injury prevention are of transcendent importance to the success of any risk management/patient injury prevention program. Once new or revised patient injury prevention systems and techniques are adopted, all relevant health care providers must become familiar with their purpose, effectiveness, and use in order to facilitate successful operation of those systems and techniques. Effective education will also serve the important purpose of motivating practitioners to active participation in patient injury prevention activities. This motivation will become manifest if the educational activities successfully demonstrate the need for physician commitment to the medically directed patient injury prevention program.

Internal education programs or information disseminated by a hospital's continuing medical education department must be considered an integral part of any risk management/patient injury prevention program. Prior to conducting these educational programs, those individuals or departments involved in directing the patient injury prevention program must determine, with the continuing medical education department (if it exists), what the educational needs of relevant hospital groups are in relation to malpractice liability and patient injury prevention. For example, two questions that must be resolved before educational programming is planned are: What knowledge do the hospital board, hospital administration, hospital medical staff, and hospital nursing staff possess about the nature, scope, causes, and frequency of hospital-generated patient injury and malpractice liability? What perceptions do these groups have regarding potential solutions to the malpractice problem? The answers to these questions will guide those constructing educational programs to fine-tune the content of the programs to the needs of specific groups within the hospital.

The subject matter of various educational programs might include:

- The magnitude of the malpractice problem: frequency and causes
- Purposes and methods of a medically directed patient injury prevention program, including incident reporting (purposes, use of guidelines for incident reporting, physician incident reporting, nonphysician incident reporting), retrospective review or medical audit, generic screening, and checklists (or procedure-indications guidelines)
- Physician responsibilities in patient injury prevention
- High-risk procedures (aimed at members of particular departments and designed to demonstrate why certain procedures generate fre-

quent and severe patient injury and malpractice liability and how these risks can be reduced)

- Programs directed at resolving problems in patient care or provider practice that have been detected by the patient injury prevention system
- Medical-legal issues for physicians (a review of physician and hospital legal accountability and liability)
- Medical-legal issues for nurses

Additionally, medicals staffs are generally receptive to continuing education programs and information on subjects such as avoiding charges of malpractice, preparing for malpractice litigation, the role of the physician-patient relationship in the prevention of malpractice claims, and the review of actual malpractice cases.

The last topic, focusing educational sessions on the review of actual malpractice cases (both those won and lost by physicians and hospitals), can be extremely effective in generating physician interest and commitment to a medically directed patient injury prevention program.

Education, whether by lecture or seminar, videotape, the routing of pertinent periodicals, or another form, can be instrumental in altering practitioner behavior that contributes to the occurrence of patient injury. As an integral component of a medically related patient injury prevention program, education can perform such critical functions as clinical training of staff; training of medical and other staff in patient injury prevention systems and techniques; and securing and maintaining active, purposeful medical staff commitment to the patient injury prevention program.

Reference

American College of Surgeons, in consultation with the Maryland Hospital Education Institute. *Patient Safety Manual: A Guide for Establishing a Patient Safety System in Your Hospital.* Chicago: ACS, 1979.

CHAPTER 8

Organization and Implementation of a Patient Injury Prevention System

The organization and implementation of a physician-related patient injury prevention system and techniques should not be a reinvention of the wheel. Much can be accomplished through the revision or modification of existing risk management and quality assurance systems. This chapter presents a series of steps designed to guide hospitals through the process necessary to establish an ongoing, effective patient injury prevention program. This "program" may merely be the incorporation of new systems and techniques into the existing risk management and quality assurance programs of hospitals. The steps that must be performed are:

- Informing and involving appropriate individuals
- Establishing a patient injury prevention work group
- Conducting an inventory of present quality assurance and risk management activities
- Analyzing the inventory results
- Identifying high-risk priorities
- Implementing systems and techniques to prevent medically related patient injury
- Defining how the patient injury prevention activities will be coordinated
- Providing for the ongoing evaluation of the system

These steps are not necessarily discrete and can be performed concurrently.

INFORMING AND INVOLVING APPROPRIATE INDIVIDUALS

The purpose of this step is to secure and maintain top-level medical and hospital management commitment to medically related patient injury prevention activities. In addition, this step requires identifying individuals within the hospital whose active support is essential to the success of patient injury prevention and malpractice loss prevention

104 / Chapter 8

activities. Without this active commitment from the medical staff, the hospital board, the administration, and nursing, the patient injury prevention program will be ineffective.

Which individuals should be involved in the program depends upon the characteristics of each hospital. The characteristics of the hospital that must be considered prior to identifying appropriate individuals include: the size of the hospital; the size of its medical staff; the organizational structure, both formal and informal; the level of functioning, effectiveness, and acceptance of current quality assurance (QA) and risk management (RM) activities; the extent of active medical staff involvement in those QA/RM activities; and the amount of turnover experienced in jobs of persons involved in QA/RM activities.

Whatever these characteristics may be, commitment should be sought from individuals whose positions require making policy decisions and the ability to implement and sustain change. These individuals should include the chief executive officer and the hospital administrator concerned with QA/RM. Also, these individuals must include the medical staff leadership engaged in QA/RM, such as the chief of staff, the medical director, and the chairmen of QA/RM-related committees. It is also critically important to inform and include those informal medical staff leaders who are committed to QA/RM purposes and activities. In this same vein, it is worthwhile to do the same (although "convert" might be more appropriate) for those informal medical staff leaders who are not familiar with, or who are opposed to, present QA/RM activities. Their commitment may make the crucial difference in gaining the support and participation of the medical staff as a whole.

It must be remembered that the thrust of these activities is the prevention of medically related patient injury. Therefore, it is critical that medical staff commitment and participation are obtained. Toward this goal, most of the initial effort should be vested into gaining and sustaining the support of the medical staff.

Also, the nursing administrator and/or the nursing QA/RM representative should be involved. Hospitals may also consider involving such other individuals as support service directors, the director of medical records, and others engaged in QA/RM activities.

Once the individuals whose commitment is necessary to the program have been identified, the next task is to secure their commitment. This can be accomplished by demonstrating that the majority of patient injuries that resulted in malpractice claims were indeed preventable and by pointing out the need for improvement in present QA/RM programs. It should also be pointed out that an effective malpractice prevention program will focus on prevention of patient injury, rather than focus on the prevention of malpractice claims.

These points can be made through educational seminars, one-on-one meetings, regularly scheduled meetings of appropriate committees, such as the medical staff executive committee, or through written communication to specific individuals or to appropriate groups or committees.

ESTABLISHING A WORK GROUP

The purpose of a work group is to review the hospital's present QA/RM programs, to plan and implement changes, to develop and implement patient injury prevention techniques, and to direct and evaluate those activities.

Those individuals who responded positively to efforts to interest them in the program should be considered for membership in the work group. The individuals in this work group for support and policy-making purposes should include key members of the medical staff, the chief executive officer or his designee, and a member of nursing administration.

Those members of the work group involved in the actual assessment of the hospital's QA/RM programs should include: at least one member of the medical staff; a member of the administration; the director of medical records; the quality assurance coordinator (or equivalent); the risk manager (or equivalent); and department/services directors, as appropriate.

The planning and implementation of changes in the QA/RM program to focus on preventing patient injuries should include those individuals listed above, with direct involvement of the medical staff through committees or through participation of the chief of staff and/or medical director *and* informal leadership of the medical staff.

CONDUCTING AN INVENTORY OF PRESENT ACTIVITIES

The main purpose of the QA/RM inventory, conducted by the work group and appropriate department heads, is to identify the level of involvement of all hospital departments and services in QA/RM. Also, the work group determines what specific patient injury prevention techniques are employed and their effectiveness.

The inventory enables a hospital to determine if its QA/RM activities are conducted as frequently as is required or as is necessary, address appropriate topics or functions, result in measurable improvements in patient care and clinical performance, and are effective in preventing medically related patient injury.

The appendix that follows this chapter presents an inventory system developed by Dixon, Lanham, and Ladenburger for the American Hospital Association's *Quality, Trending, and Management for the '80s: A Hospitalwide Quality Assurance Seminar.* This detailed inventory system will permit each hospital to assess its entire QA program, as well as its departmental quality assurance activities.

ANALYZING INVENTORY FINDINGS

The actual conduct of the inventory itself will supply the work group with valuable information regarding the functioning and effectiveness of QA/RM activities. Once the inventory is completed, the work group must analyze the findings. The purpose of the inventory analysis is to study the effectiveness of QA/RM activities in preventing medically related patient injury, improving the quality of patient care, and minimizing the potential for malpractice claims and loss. In addition, the inventory analysis identifies activities or methods that are duplicative and unnecessary and indicates what new methods or techniques should be instituted to improve deficient areas.

The inventory analysis consists of several different activities. These include a comparison of all department/service evaluation and problem prevention and solving activities and also focuses on the integrity of information flow. For example, a department may be successfully identifying urgent problems in patient care that may manifest later as compensable patient injuries; but this information may not generate any corrective action. The inventory analysis should screen for and identify such points of information inhibition and then clarify ways of improving this critical information flow. The inventory analysis should also include a comparison of actual malpractice claims with the QA/RM review activities of the areas that generated the claims. If those patient injuries that later resulted in malpractice claims went undetected by the various review activities (including incident reporting), then a serious problem exists. The inventory analysis will therefore focus also on data source utilization.

In general, the inventory and analysis steps provide the work group and the hospital with detailed feedback regarding the strengths, weaknesses, and overall effectiveness of its quality assurance and risk management process. These steps therefore suggest actions to improve the functioning and effectiveness of those programs. These two steps also identify methods or techniques that can be upgraded or initiated to function as effective medically related patient injury prevention systems.

IDENTIFYING HIGH-RISK PRIORITIES

This step requires the development of an accurate data base for identifying departments, areas, or procedures that are most likely to generate medically related patient injuries. The inventory and inventory analysis are useful in compiling this internal data base, but the work group must also rely upon other internal and external data sources. The purpose of this step is to identify those departments, areas, or procedures that—because of the degree of risk they pose to patients—must be the immediate focus of specific methods and techniques to prevent the occurrence of medically related patient injury.

The first task in developing high-risk resolution priorities is to review pertinent external data sources. Nationwide data will impart an understanding of which medical specialties and procedures and which hospital departments and areas generally represent high-risk areas of patient injury. Chapter 5 of this book provides an overview of and references to the major external data sources and the general areas, departments, specialties, and procedures that carry high risk of injury.

The second task of this step is to analyze internal hospital data sources to gain an exact understanding of where the greatest areas of risk of patient injury are for each hospital. To accomplish this task, the work group must combine pertinent results of the inventory analysis with other internal sources of information regarding the occurrence of patient injuries and the filing of malpractice claims. A few of these sources of information include:

- Review of incident reports to determine hospital areas or departments where serious incidents are most frequent
- Mortality review
- Actual malpractice claims made against the hospital, a hospital employee, or a member of the hospital medical staff
- Medical care evaluation studies
- Continuous monitors
- Committee minutes
- Fiscal intermediaries' reports
- Department head interviews
- Staff interviews
- Patient complaints
- Patient representative reports
- Patient questionnaires
- Readmission rates
- Employee exit interviews
- Ancillary services review
- Operating room schedule
- Continuing medical and professional education evaluations
- Patient transfer data
- Comparison of bylaws statements against actual practices or procedures
- Checking credentials files against operating room schedule
- Analysis of retrospective denials of payments

The work group should utilize any internal data source that may possibly uncover valuable information about problem areas in patient care.

Once the work group has reviewed and compared external and internal data and has a list of hospital areas or procedures that carry high risk of patient injury, it must establish priorities or risk reduction. These priorities can be established by using the following formula:

> The greatest priority for immediate establishment of patient injury prevention techniques will be the problem with:
>
> > the greatest frequency
> > +
> > the greatest potential severity of injury to patients
> > +
> > the potential for substantial reduction of risk to patients

Using this "formula," the work group can effectively determine which areas, departments, or procedures warrant immediate establishment of patient injury prevention techniques.

IMPLEMENTING SYSTEMS AND TECHNIQUES

Once high-risk areas have been identified, patient injury prevention techniques must be directed at those areas. The task of the work group is to determine which patient injury prevention systems and techniques are appropriate to the specific areas or departments identified. Chapter 6 recommends a series of techniques and systems that may be applicable for use in particular areas or departments. In addition, the work group may modify existing quality assurance and risk management activities for more refined and effective use as medically related patient injury prevention techniques and systems.

The work group will also, when appropriate, devise and implement new systems and techniques aimed at preventing medically related patient injuries. These new techniques will be developed in response to areas of risk and need that have been identified by the inventory analysis and the establishment of high risk priorities.

DEFINING ACTIVITY COORDINATION

This step requires consideration of how to effectively coordinate and organize medically related patient injury prevention activities in relation to the quality assurance and risk management functions.

The inventory and inventory analysis will provide detailed assessment of the effectiveness and efficiency of the present coordinating function for the QA/RM programs. On the basis of the results of the inventory analysis, the work group, the administration, the chief of the medical staff or the medical director, the QA coordinator (or equivalent), and the risk manager (or equivalent) must decide whether to maintain or to revise the present QA/RM functions. Inherent to this decision will be the incorporation of the patient injury prevention activities within the scope of either the quality assurance or risk management programs, or both.

These decisions must be made by each hospital individually, and hospitals should refrain from adopting organizational models developed by outside sources. The organizational model and coordinating function for these activities must be developed internally by each hospital to truly reflect and address those characteristics that make each hospital unique. The type of organization and coordination is, in itself, unimportant. What is of transcendent importance is the effective prevention of medically related patient injury. The analysis of the effectiveness of the quality assurance and risk management coordinating function will identify any problems in organization, information flow, corrective action, and reduction of patient injury that existed in the past. These problems must then be corrected by modifying the present coordinating function or by instituting alternatives. Once an organizational and coordinating function is chosen, it should be documented in a plan that outlines the flow of information; the data sources to be used; the lines of authority, accountability, and communication; and the methods and activities employed to prevent medically related patient injury.

PROVIDING FOR ONGOING EVALUATION

The purpose of this final step is to ensure that the patient injury prevention system is ongoing and effective, once it has been established. This evaluation may be performed in several ways, once the coordinating function of the QA/RM programs has been revised to incorporate patient injury prevention activities. After a new system has functioned for about six months, the steps of conducting an inventory and the inventory analysis may be selectively repeated by the work group or coordinating authority. This repetition of conducting the inventory and the inventory analysis performs several functions: it confirms that deficiencies identified by the last inventory have been corrected; it verifies the functioning of new patient injury prevention activities; and it indicates the effectiveness of those new activities in preventing medically related patient injury.

Another, more ongoing, method of reappraisal is the review of malpractice claims against incident reports and other detection activities. If the system is functioning effectively, incident reports will have been filed for the majority (greater than 70 percent) of patient injuries that resulted in a malpractice claim. The magnitude of the disparity between incident reports and patient injuries resulting in malpractice claims will be a valuable indicator as to the effectiveness of the incident reporting system specifically and of the patient injury prevention activities in general.

In addition, areas that generated many medically related patient injuries prior to the institution of patient injury prevention activities should be evaluated to determine if there is a measurable and significant decline in the frequency and severity of patient injury. This is the real test of the effectiveness of a patient injury prevention program and quantifies the progress made toward the goal of preventing as many patient injuries as possible.

The ongoing evaluation of these activities enables each hospital to continually fine-tune them, thereby increasing their efficiency and maximizing their effectiveness in promptly detecting high-risk situations and in preventing medically related patient injuries.

Appendix:

Quality Assurance
Program Inventory

This inventory system was developed by Dixon, Lanham, and Ladenburger for the American Hospital Association's *Quality, Trending, and Management for the 80's: A Hospitalwide Quality Assurance Seminar.* It is intended for use by hospitals to survey their quality assurance programs, and its use is recommended for organizing and implementing a patient injury prevention system, especially for conducting an inventory of present QA/RM activities and analyzing inventory results.

Department Service Inventory

Directions: The following pages contain questions for each hospital department/service relating to the department's or service's participation in quality assurance activities. Questions are related to requirements specified in the *Accreditation Manual for Hospitals,* 1980 edition, and are designed to facilitate a hospital's assessment of its present quality assurance activities.

The questions on pages 137 and 138 are intended to identify how each department or service contributes to the hospital's overall quality assurance program. The pages should be duplicated for use by all hospital departments and services. The questions should be answered for *each* department or service included on pages 113 through 136.

Each of the following pages may be distributed to appropriate department or service directors for completion or may be completed by the hospital's quality assurance work group through personal or telephone interviews with department/service directors or review of available department/service documentation.

ANESTHESIA SERVICES

QUESTION	YES NO N/A ?	NOTES

Is documentation available to demonstrate the following about anesthesia services review?

1. Conducted at least quarterly?   YES NO N/A ?
2. Uses preestablished criteria?   YES NO N/A ?
3. Includes care provided in:
   a. Surgical areas?   YES NO N/A ?
   b. Obstetrical areas?   YES NO N/A ?
   c. Emergency areas?   YES NO N/A ?
   d. Ambulatory care areas?   YES NO N/A ?
   e. Psychiatric care areas?   YES NO N/A ?
   f. Special procedure areas?   YES NO N/A ?
4. Includes care provided by:
   a. Anesthesiologists?   YES NO N/A ?
   b. Other qualified physicians?   YES NO N/A ?
   c. Dentists?   YES NO N/A ?
   d. Nurse anesthetists?   YES NO N/A ?
   e. Individuals in an approved training program?   YES NO N/A ?
   f. Individuals associated with or employed by a surgeon or group of surgeons rather than by the hospital?   YES NO N/A ?
5. Director of the anesthesia department/service assumes responsibility for the quality assurance activities?   YES NO N/A ?
6. Reports include:
   a. Findings of evaluation?   YES NO N/A ?
   b. All resultant action?   YES NO N/A ?
   c. Follow-up?   YES NO N/A ?
7. Results have been used in identifying or conducting any education programs?   YES NO N/A ?
8. Person retrieving data
9. Location of files.

DIETETIC SERVICES

QUESTION	YES NO N/A ?	NOTES
Is documentation available to demonstrate the following about dietetic services review:		
1. Conducted at least annually?	YES NO N/A ?	
2. Uses preestablished criteria?	YES NO N/A ?	
3. Uses the medical record?	YES NO N/A ?	
4. Includes nutritional care provided to:		
a. Inpatients?	YES NO N/A ?	
b. Ambulatory care patients?	YES NO N/A ?	
c. Home care program patients?	YES NO N/A ?	
5. Includes dietetic services provided by outside sources?	YES NO N/A ?	
6. Includes input from the:		
a. Medical staff?	YES NO N/A ?	
b. Nursing staff?	YES NO N/A ?	
c. Dietetic staff?	YES NO N/A ?	
7. Director of the dietetic department/services assumes responsibility for the quality assurance activities?	YES NO N/A ?	
8. If the director is not a qualified dietitian, a qualified dietitian provides consultation in the performance of quality assurance activities?	YES NO N/A ?	
9. Results have been used in identifying or conducting any education programs?	YES NO N/A ?	
10. Person retrieving/collating review quality assurance data		
11. Location of department/ service quality assurance files		

EMERGENCY SERVICES

QUESTION	YES NO N/A ?	NOTES

Is documentation available to demonstrate the following about emergency services review:

1. Conducted at least monthly? — YES NO N/A ?
2. Uses preestablished criteria? — YES NO N/A ?
3. Uses the medical record? — YES NO N/A ?
4. Includes care provided to individuals who:
   a. Are dead on arrival? — YES NO N/A ?
   b. Die in the emergency department service area? — YES NO N/A ?
   c. Die within 24 hours of admission from the emergency department/ service area? — YES NO N/A ?
5. Includes daily review of at least a sample of emergency medical records from the previous 24 hours to assess adequacy of:
   a. Service rendered? — YES NO N/A ?
   b. Documentation? — YES NO N/A ?
6. Director of the emergency department/service (or emergency care committee chairman) assumes responsibility for the quality assurance activities? — YES NO N/A ?
7. Appropriate action has been taken on the findings? — YES NO N/A ?
8. Results have been used in identifying or conducting any education programs? — YES NO N/A ?
9. Person retrieving/collating quality assurance data
10. Location of department/ service quality assurance files

HOME CARE SERVICES

QUESTION	YES NO N/A ?	NOTES

Is documentation available to demonstrate the following about home care service review:

1. Conducted at least annually to evaluate:
   a. The program objectives and the degree of their fulfillment? — YES NO N/A ?
   b. Quality and appropriateness of care provided? — YES NO N/A ?
   c. Accessibility, timeliness, and need for services? — YES NO N/A ?
2. Active and closed record review at least quarterly by health professionals representing the scope of services provided to include:
   a. Whether established policies are being followed? — YES NO N/A ?
   b. The adequacy of records for use in patient care evaluation? — YES NO N/A ?
3. Patient care plans reviewed at least once every 60 days and include review of all medications that a patient is known to be taking? — YES NO N/A ?
4. A multidisciplinary committee composed of at least one physician, one nurse, and the program director assumes responsibility for the program evaluation? — YES NO N/A ?
5. Recommendations have been:
   a. Documented? — YES NO N/A ?
   b. Reported in accordance with hospital policy? — YES NO N/A ?
6. Person retrieving data
7. Location of files

HOSPITAL-SPONSORED AMBULATORY CARE SERVICES

QUESTION	YES NO N/A ?	NOTES

Is documentation available to
demonstrate the following about
hospital-sponsored ambulatory
care services review:

1. Conducted at least
   semi-annually?   YES NO N/A ?
2. Uses preestablished criteria?   YES NO N/A ?
3. Uses the medical record?   YES NO N/A ?
4. Includes ambulatory services
   provided by:
   a. Hospital staff?   YES NO N/A ?
   b. Outside sources under the
      sponsorship of the hospital?   YES NO N/A ?
5. Director of the ambulatory
   care department/service and
   the directors of other hospital
   departments/services wherein
   ambulatory care services are
   provided assume responsibility
   for the quality assurance
   activities?   YES NO N/A ?
6. Appropriate action has been
   taken on the findings?   YES NO N/A ?
7. Results have been used in
   identifying or conducting
   any education programs?   YES NO N/A ?
8. Reports include:
   a. Findings of evaluation?   YES NO N/A ?
   b. Actions taken?   YES NO N/A ?
9. Person retrieving/collating
   quality assurance data
10. Location of department/
    service quality assurance files

INFECTION CONTROL

QUESTION	YES NO N/A ?	NOTES

Is documentation available to
demonstrate the following about
the infection control program:

1. Review at least bimonthly?   YES NO N/A ?
2. Review includes:
    a. Infections within the
       hospital, particularly with
       regard to their proper
       management and their
       epidemic potential?   YES NO N/A ?
    b. Any cultures of personnel
       or the environment required
       by the hospital, medical
       staff, or local, state, or
       federal agencies or
       regulations?   YES NO N/A ?
    c. Results of antimicrobial
       susceptibility/resistance
       trend studies?   YES NO N/A ?
    d. Proposals and protocols for
       all special infection control
       studies, including any
       subsequent findings?   YES NO N/A ?
    e. Medical records reflecting
       the presence of infections
       that were not reported in
       the final diagnosis?   YES NO N/A ?

INFECTION CONTROL (cont.)

QUESTION	YES NO N/A ?	NOTES
f. Necropsy reports when undiagnosed antemortem infections are discovered?	YES NO N/A ?	
g. Pertinent related findings from other hospital committees?	YES NO N/A ?	
3. A multidiciplinary committee including representation from the medical staff, administration, nursing, and microbiology, when available, assumes responsibility for monitoring the program?	YES NO N/A ?	
4. Findings and recommendations are reported to the:		
a. Executive committee?	YES NO N/A ?	
b. Chief executive officer?	YES NO N/A ?	
c. Director of nursing?	YES NO N/A ?	
5. Results have been used in identifying or conducting any education programs?	YES NO N/A ?	
6. Person retrieving/collating data		
7. Location of program files		

MEDICAL STAFF: TISSUE REVIEW FUNCTION

QUESTION	YES NO N/A ?	NOTES

Is documentation available to
demonstrate the following about
tissue review:

1. Conducted at least monthly?   YES NO N/A ?
2. Includes cases in which:
   a. A specimen (tissue or
   nontissue) was removed?   YES NO N/A ?
   b. No specimen was removed?   YES NO N/A ?
3. Includes:
   a. Indications for surgery?   YES NO N/A ?
   b. Major discrepancies
   between preoperative and
   postoperative diagnoses?   YES NO N/A ?
4. The surgical department/
   service or a medical staff
   committee assumes
   responsibility for surgical
   case review?   YES NO N/A ?
5. Appropriate action has been
   taken on the findings?   YES NO N/A ?
6. Results are used as part of the
   reappraisal mechanism, when
   appropriate?   YES NO N/A ?
7. Reports include:
   a. Results of all review
   performance?   YES NO N/A ?
   b. Actions taken?   YES NO N/A ?
8. Person retrieving/collating
   data
9. Location of review files

MEDICAL STAFF: PHARMACY AND THERAPEUTICS FUNCTION

QUESTION	YES NO N/A ?	NOTES

Is documentation available to
demonstrate the following about
the pharamacy and therapeutics
function:

1. Conducted at least quarterly?   YES NO N/A ?
2. Includes:
   a. Development and
      surveillance of established
      policies and procedures
      relating to selection,
      intrahospital distribution
      and handling, and safe
      administration of drugs?   YES NO N/A ?
   b. Development of a
      formulary?   YES NO N/A ?
3. Includes review of:
   a. Drug utilization?   YES NO N/A ?
   b. The formulary for
      currentness at stated
      intervals?   YES NO N/A ?
   c. All untoward drug
      reactions?   YES NO N/A ?
   d. Approval of all protocols
      for use of investigational
      or experimental drugs?   YES NO N/A ?
4. Includes participation of the:
   a. Medical staff?   YES NO N/A ?
   b. Nursing staff?   YES NO N/A ?
   c. Pharmaceutical
      department/service?   YES NO N/A ?
   d. Administration?   YES NO N/A ?
5. Results are used as part of the
   reappraisal mechanism?   YES NO N/A ?
6. Reports include:
   a. Results of all evaluations?   YES NO N/A ?
   b. Actions taken?   YES NO N/A ?
7. Person retrieving data
8. Location of review files

MEDICAL STAFF: MEDICAL RECORD FUNCTION

QUESTION	YES NO N/A ?	NOTES

Is documentation available to
demonstrate the following about
the medical record function:

1. Conducted at least quarterly?   YES NO N/A ?
2. Includes records of:
   a. Inpatients?   YES NO N/A ?
   b. Ambulatory care patients?   YES NO N/A ?
   c. Emergency patients?   YES NO N/A ?
   d. Home care patients?   YES NO N/A ?
3. Includes review of records:
   a. Timely completion?   YES NO N/A ?
   b. Clinical pertinence?   YES NO N/A ?
   c. Adequacy for use in quality
      assessment?   YES NO N/A ?
   d. Adequacy as medical-legal
      document?   YES NO N/A ?
   e. Reflection of condition and
      progress of patient?   YES NO N/A ?
   f. Reflection of results of all
      tests and therapy given?   YES NO N/A ?
   g. Reflection of safe transfer
      of physician responsibility,
      if necessary?   YES NO N/A ?

MEDICAL STAFF: MEDICAL RECORD FUNCTION (cont.)

QUESTION	YES NO N/A ?	NOTES
4. Includes:		
a. Format of completed records?	YES NO N/A ?	
b. Forms used in records?	YES NO N/A ?	
c. Use of microfilming?	YES NO N/A ?	
5. Includes participation of the:		
a. Medical staff?	YES NO N/A ?	
b. Nursing service/ department?	YES NO N/A ?	
c. Medical record department?	YES NO N/A ?	
6. Appropriate action has been taken on findings?	YES NO N/A ?	
7. Results are used as part of the reappraisal mechanism, when appropriate?	YES NO N/A ?	
8. Reports include:		
a. Results of all evaluations?	YES NO N/A ?	
b. Actions taken?	YES NO N/A ?	
9. Person retrieving/collating data		
10. Location of review files		

MEDICAL STAFF: BLOOD UTILIZATION REVIEW

QUESTION	YES NO N/A ?	NOTES
Is documentation available to demonstrate the following about blood utilization review:		
1. Conducted at least quarterly?	YES NO N/A ?	
2. Includes records of:		
a. Inpatients?	YES NO N/A ?	
b. Ambulatory care patients?	YES NO N/A ?	
c. Emergency patients?	YES NO N/A ?	
3. Includes:		
a. Blood transfusions for proper utilization?	YES NO N/A ?	
b. The amount of blood requested, used, and wastage?	YES NO N/A ?	
c. The use of whole blood versus component blood elements?	YES NO N/A ?	
d. Each actual or suspected transfusion reaction?	YES NO N/A ?	
4. A separate committee, group, or individual of the medical staff; an existing medical staff committee; or individual clinical departments/services assume responsibility for blood utilization review?	YES NO N/A ?	
5. All actual or suspected transfusions are documented?	YES NO N/A ?	
6. Results have been used as part of the reappraisal mechanism, when appropriate?	YES NO N/A ?	
7. Person retrieving/collating data		
8. Location of review files		

MEDICAL STAFF: ANTIBIOTIC USAGE REVIEW

QUESTION	YES NO N/A ?	NOTES

Is documentation available to demonstrate the following about antibiotic usage review:

1. Conducted on an ongoing basis? — YES NO N/A ?
2. Includes the prophylactic use of antibiotics for:
   a. Inpatients? — YES NO N/A ?
   b. Ambulatory care patients? — YES NO N/A ?
   c. Emergency patients? — YES NO N/A ?
3. Criteria for the prophylactic and therapeutic use of antibiotics are established in problem areas? — YES NO N/A ?
4. Departures from established criteria are reviewed in a timely manner? — YES NO N/A ?
5. Review is under the direction of the medical staff? — YES NO N/A ?
6. Appropriate action has been taken on the findings? — YES NO N/A ?
7. Results are used as part of the reappraisal mechanism, when appropriate? — YES NO N/A ?
8. Reports include:
   a. Findings of review activities? — YES NO N/A ?
   b. Actions taken? — YES NO N/A ?
   c. Follow-up program? — YES NO N/A ?
9. Person retrieving/collating data
10. Location of review files

MEDICAL STAFF: OTHER REVIEW,
EVALUATION, AND MONITORING FUNCTIONS

QUESTION	YES NO N/A ?	NOTES

Is documentation available to
demonstrate the following:

1. Continuous monitoring of
   patient care elements identified
   in the medical staff or clinical
   department/service rules and
   regulations?   YES NO N/A ?
2. Results of monitoring are used
   as part of the reappraisal
   mechanism, when
   appropriate?   YES NO N/A ?
3. Person retrieving/collating
   data
4. Location of review and
   monitoring files

NUCLEAR MEDICINE SERVICES

QUESTION	YES NO N/A ?	NOTES

Is documentation available to demonstrate the following:

1. The director of nuclear medicine department/service reviews the quality, safety, and appropriateness of nuclear medicine services provided?   YES NO N/A ?
2. Person collating/retrieving review data
3. Location of review files

NURSING SERVICES

QUESTION	YES NO N/A ?	NOTES

Is documentation available to demonstrate the following about nursing care review:

1. Conducted at least quarterly?   YES NO N/A ?
2. Uses written criteria?   YES NO N/A ?
3. Includes care provided by nursing personnel who are not hospital employees?   YES NO N/A ?
4. Includes nursing monitoring functions?   YES NO N/A ?
5. Includes participation of nursing staff who provide patient care?   YES NO N/A ?
6. Nurse administrator assumes responsibility for the quality assurance activities?   YES NO N/A ?
7. Pertinent findings of the review are disseminated within the nursing department/ service?   YES NO N/A ?
8. Appropriate action has been taken on results of review/monitoring activities?   YES NO N/A ?
9. Results have been used in identifying or conducting any education programs?   YES NO N/A ?
10. Person retrieving/collating quality assurance data
11. Location of department/ service quality assurance files

PATHOLOGY AND MEDICAL LABORATORY SERVICES

QUESTION	YES NO N/A ?	NOTES
Is documentation available to demonstrate the following:		
1. Quality and appropriateness of pathology and medical laboratory services is reviewed?	YES NO N/A ?	
2. Director of the pathology and medical laboratory services assumes responsibility for quality assurance activities?	YES NO N/A ?	
3. Results of the review of pathology and medical laboratory services have been used in identifying or conducting education programs?	YES NO N/A ?	
4. Person retrieving/collating evaluation data		
5. Location of department/ service evaluation files		

PHARMACEUTICAL SERVICES

QUESTION	YES NO N/A ?	NOTES

Is documentation available to demonstrate the following:

1. Director of the pharmaceutical department/service participates in quality assurance activities that relate to drug utilization and effectiveness?   YES NO N/A ?

2. Director of the pharmaceutical department/service is an active member of the pharmacy and therapeutics committee?   YES NO N/A ?

3. Person retrieving/collating drug utilization-related data

4. Location of drug utilization and other drug-related quality assurance files

RADIOLOGY SERVICES

QUESTION	YES NO N/A ?	NOTES
Is documentation available to demonstrate the following:		
1. Quality and appropriateness radiological services is reviewed?	YES NO N/A ?	
2. A quality control program:		
a. Minimizes unnecessary duplication of radiographic studies?	YES NO N/A ?	
b. Maximizes the quality of diagnostic information available?	YES NO N/A ?	
3. Director of the radiology department/service assumes responsibility for the quality assurance and control activities?	YES NO N/A ?	
4. Results of the evaluation of radiological services have been used in identifying or conducting education programs?	YES NO N/A ?	
5. Person retrieving/collating review data		
6. Location of department/ service review files		

REHABILITATION PROGRAMS/SERVICES

QUESTION	YES NO N/A ?	NOTES
Is documentation available to demonstrate the following about rehabilitation programs/services review:		
1. Conducted at least quarterly?	YES NO N/A ?	
2. Uses predetermined criteria?	YES NO N/A ?	
3. Includes rehabilitation services provided by outside sources?	YES NO N/A ?	
4. Includes participation of:		
a. Medical staff?	YES NO N/A ?	
b. Rehabilitation personnel?	YES NO N/A ?	
5. Director of the rehabilitation program/services assumes responsibility for the quality assurance activities?	YES NO N/A ?	
6. Results have been used in identifying or conducting any education programs?	YES NO N/A ?	
7. Person retrieving/collating quality assurance data		
8. Location of department/ service quality assurance files		

RESPIRATORY CARE SERVICES

QUESTION	YES NO N/A ?	NOTES

Is documentation available to demonstrate the following about respiratory care services review:

1. Conducted at least quarterly? — YES NO N/A ?
2. Uses preestablished criteria? — YES NO N/A ?
3. Uses the medical record? — YES NO N/A ?
4. Includes records of:
   a. Inpatients? — YES NO N/A ?
   b. Ambulatory care patients? — YES NO N/A ?
   c. Home care patients? — YES NO N/A ?
5. Includes:
   a. Indications for use? — YES NO N/A ?
   b. Effectiveness of treatment? — YES NO N/A ?
   c. Adverse effects requiring discontinuance of treatment? — YES NO N/A ?
   d. Necessity for services having the highest utilization rate? — YES NO N/A ?
6. Includes respiratory care services provided by outside sources? — YES NO N/A ?
7. Includes input of:
   a. Medical staff? — YES NO N/A ?
   b. Respiratory care personnel? — YES NO N/A ?
8. Physician director of the respiratory care department/ service assumes responsibility for the quality assurance activities? — YES NO N/A ?
9. Results have been used in identifying or conducting any education programs? — YES NO N/A ?
10. Person retrieving/collating quality assurance data
11. Location of department/ service quality assurance files

SOCIAL WORK SERVICES

QUESTION	YES NO N/A ?	NOTES

Is documentation available to demonstrate the following about social work services review:

1. Conducted at least semiannually?   YES NO N/A ?
2. Uses preestablished criteria?   YES NO N/A ?
3. Uses the medical record?   YES NO N/A ?
4. Includes records of:
   a. Inpatients?   YES NO N/A ?
   b. Ambulatory care patients?   YES NO N/A ?
   c. Emergency care patients?   YES NO N/A ?
   d. Home care patients?   YES NO N/A ?
5. Includes:
   a. Indications for providing social work services?   YES NO N/A ?
   b. Effectiveness of social work interventions?   YES NO N/A ?
   c. Appropriateness and effectiveness of patient transfer to long-term care?   YES NO N/A ?
   d. Appropriateness and effectiveness of patient placement in the home with supportive services?   YES NO N/A ?
6. Includes social work services provided by outside sources?   YES NO N/A ?
7. Director of social work services responsible for quality assurance activities?   YES NO N/A ?
8. Appropriate action has been taken on the findings?   YES NO N/A ?
9. Results have been used in identifying or conducting any education programs?   YES NO N/A ?
10. Person retrieving data
11. Location of files

SPECIAL CARE UNITS

QUESTION	YES NO N/A ?	NOTES

Is documentation available to demonstrate the following about special care units review:

1. Conducted at least quarterly?   YES NO N/A ?
2. Director of each special care unit assumes responsibility for the quality assurance activities?   YES NO N/A ?
3. If the unit is a multi-purpose special care unit, a multidisciplinary committee of the medical staff assumes responsibility for the quality assurance activities?   YES NO N/A ?
4. Appropriate action is taken on findings of review activities?   YES NO N/A ?
5. Results have been used in identifying or conducting any education programs?   YES NO N/A ?
6. Person retrieving/collating quality assurance data
7. Location of unit(s) quality assurance files

UTILIZATION REVIEW

QUESTION	YES NO N/A ?	NOTES

Is documentation available to demonstrate the following:

1. Findings of the following activities are examined to identify utilization problems:
   a. Profile analysis?   YES NO N/A ?
   b. Patient care evaulation
      studies?   YES NO N/A ?
   c. Surgical case review?   YES NO N/A ?
   d. Antibiotic usage review?   YES NO N/A ?
   e. Blood utilization review?   YES NO N/A ?
   f. Infection control activities?   YES NO N/A ?
   g. Hospital-specific
      reimbursement agency
      utilization reports?   YES NO N/A ?
2. Location of files of documentation listed above

DEPARTMENT/SERVICE SUMMARY INVENTORY

NOTE: Each of the following questions refers to a characteristic of the hospital's overall quality assurance program.

QUESTION	YES NO N/A ?	NOTES

Is documentation available to demonstrate the following:

1. FORMALIZED: Findings of quality assurance activities are reported to the:
   a. Medical staff?   YES NO N/A ?
   b. Chief executive officer?   YES NO N/A ?
   c. Governing body?   YES NO N/A ?
2. PROBLEM-FOCUSED: Problems that have been addressed in the quality assurance activities are listed or documented in some fashion?   YES NO N/A ?
3. EFFECTIVE: Identified problems have been reduced or eliminated?   YES NO N/A ?
4. WELL DEFINED: Mechanisms used to review and evaluate patient care are defined?   YES NO N/A ?
5. ORGANIZED: A written definition exists of the role(s) of the individuals and/or committee involved in quality assurance?   YES NO N/A ?
6. COMPREHENSIVE: The care provided by all practitioners, including physicians and nonphysicians, is evaluated as part of the quality assurance activities?   YES NO N/A ?

DEPARTMENT/SERVICE SUMMARY INVENTORY (cont.)

QUESTION	YES NO N/A ?	NOTES
7. **INTEGRATED/ COORDINATED:** The role of this department's/service's quality assurance in the overall hospital quality assurance program is defined?	YES NO N/A ?	
8. REAPPRAISED: There is annual reappraisal of the quality assurance activities:		
a. Performance at required intervals? (as stated in accreditation standards)	YES NO N/A ?	
b. Comprehensiveness? (see question 6)	YES NO N/A ?	
c. Effectiveness? (see question 3)	YES NO N/A ?	
d. Cost efficiency? (see question 10)	YES NO N/A ?	
9. FLEXIBLE: The quality of care is evaluated through any mechanism other than retrospective audit?	YES NO N/A ?	
10. COST-EFFICIENT: Are any of the quality assurance activities performed by this department/ service duplicated by someone else in the hospital?	YES NO N/A ?	

Overall Quality Assurance Program Inventory

Directions: The following pages are designed to facilitate a hospital's assessment of its present *overall* quality assurance program.

The chart on the next page may be completed by the hospital's quality assurance work group or by an individual designated by the group. The chart is completed by filling in the answers given by each hospital department or service for the questions given on pages 137 and 138.

The questions on pages 141 and 142 relate to hospital functions that support the development of an overall quality assurance program. They should be answered by the quality assurance work group or its designee.

INVENTORY SUMMARY

Fill in responses from completed copies of pages 137 and 138.

Department/Service	1. FORMALIZED	2. PROBLEM-FOCUSED	3. EFFECTIVE	4. WELL-DEFINED	5. ORGANIZED	6. COMPRE-HENSIVE	7. INTEGRATED COORDINATED	8. REAPPRAISED	9. FLEXIBLE	10. COST-EFFICIENT
Anesthesia Services										
Dietetic Services										
Emergency Services										
Home Care Services										
Hospital-Sponsored Ambulatory Care Services										
Infection Control										
Tissue Review										
Pharmacy and Therapeutics Function										
Medical Record Function										
Blood Utilization Review										
Antibiotic Usage Review										
Nuclear Medicine Services										
Nursing Services										
Pathology and Medical Laboratory Services										
Pharmaceutical Service										
Radiology Services										
Rehabilitation Programs/Services										
Respiratory Care Service										
Social Work Services										
Special Care Units										
Utilization Review										

QUALITY ASSURANCE PROGRAM

NOTE: *Some of the following questions refer to characteristics of the hospital's quality assurance program; others refer to requirements contained in the* Accreditation Manual for Hospitals, *1980 edition of the Joint Commission on Accreditation of Hospitals.*

QUESTION	YES NO N/A ?	NOTES

Is documentation available to demonstrate the following:

1. FORMALIZED: The hospital governing body has established a quality assurance program? — YES NO N/A ?

2. FORMALIZED: The governing body has assured the provision of administrative assistance and medical record department services to support the quality assurance program? — YES NO N/A ?

3. FORMALIZED: The governing body has specified the nature and frequency of reports it receives on the hospital quality assurance activities? — YES NO N/A ?

4. PROBLEM-FOCUSED: Incident/occurrence reports are reviewed through the quality assurance program to identify actual or potential patient care problems? — YES NO N/A ?

5. PROBLEM-FOCUSED/ COST-EFFICIENT: Medical records are not used as the sole data source to review quality of patient care? — YES NO N/A ?

6. WELL-DEFINED: The hospital has a written quality assurance program plan? — YES NO N/A ?

QUALITY ASSURANCE PROGRAM

QUESTION	YES NO N/A ?	NOTES
7. WELL-DEFINED: The quality assurance program has specifically defined terminology used to describe studies performed or methods employed in quality assessment activities?	YES NO N/A ?	
8. ORGANIZED: The quality assurance program is administered by a committee, group, or individual?	YES NO N/A ?	
9. REAPPRAISAL: The overall quality assurance program is reappraised annually?	YES NO N/A ?	
10. FLEXIBLE: The methods used to review and evaluate patient care are tailored to meet the specific needs of the hospital?	YES NO N/A ?	

Quality Assurance Program
Needs and Priorities

Directions: Use the following pages to list tentative needs and priorities for improvement of the hospital quality assurance program. Needs and priorities may be developed by the quality assurance work group or by an individual designated by the group.

QUALITY ASSURANCE PROGRAM NEEDS

DEPARTMENT/SERVICE	NEEDS
Anesthesia	
Dietetic	
Emergency	
Home Care	
Hospital-Sponsored Ambulatory Care	
Infection Control	
Tissue Review	
Pharmacy and Therapeutics	
Medical Record	
Blood Utilization	
Antibiotic Usage Review	
Other Medical Staff Monitors	
Nuclear Medicine	
Nursing	
Pathology and Medical Laboratory	
Pharmaceutical	
Radiology	
Rehabilitation	
Respiratory Care	
Social Work	
Special Care Units	
Utilization Review	

QUALITY ASSURANCE PROGRAM NEEDS (cont.)

DEPARTMENT/SERVICE   **NEEDS**

QUALITY ASSURANCE PROGRAM PRIORITIES

_____

_____
_____
_____
_____
_____
_____
_____
_____
_____
_____
_____
_____
_____
_____
_____
_____
_____
_____
_____
_____
_____
_____
_____
_____
_____